AF539632

MASKED INVERSION IN FRENCH

MASKED INVERSION IN FRENCH

Paul M. Postal

The University of Chicago Press
Chicago and London

Paul M. Postal is a member of the research staff at IBM's T. J. Watson Research Center. He is the author of ten books including *An Integrated Theory of Linguistic Description, Constituent Structure, Cross-over Phenomena, On Raising,* and *Arc Pair Grammar.*

The University of Chicago Press, Chicago 60637
The University of Chicago Press, Ltd., London

Printed in the United States of America

98 97 96 95 94 93 92 91 90 89   54321

Library of Congress Cataloging-in-Publication Data

Postal, Paul Martin, 1936–
Masked inversion in French / Paul M. Postal.
p.   cm.
Bibliography: p.
Includes index.
ISBN 0-226-67569-6
1. French language—Word order. 2. French language—Syntax.
I. Title.
PC2380.P66 1989
445—dc19   88-21794
CIP

Contents

Preface

This study of natural language (henceforth NL) grammatical structure begins with consideration of a well-known apparent anomaly in French grammar, the fact that in the so-called causative or *faire* construction a handful of verbs (hereafter Vs) appear to violate a rule precluding NON-THIRD PERSON or reflexive direct objects in a wide class of transitive structures. The NORMAL situation is illustrated in (A).

(A) a. Le directeur le/la/les fera choisir à Marie.
"The director will make Marie choose him/her/them."
b. * Le directeur se/me/te/nous/vous fera choisir à Marie.
"The director will make/have Marie choose himself/me/you/us/you (formal or plural)."

But with a few Vs, most notably *connaître,* the sentences (Bb) are as grammatical as those of (Ba).

(B) a. Le directeur le/la/les fera connaître à Marie.
"The director will make/have Marie know him/her/them."
b. Le directeur se/me/te/nous/vous fera connaître à Marie.
"The director will make/have Marie know himself/me/you/us/you."

Before I continue, a word is in order about the glosses used in this work for *connaître,* whose most neutral meaning is 'know', but which in certain cases can or even must mean 'meet' or 'have social relations with'. I have systematically glossed this V as 'know', except in a few cases where that seems absurd; in those, the gloss is expanded to include 'meet'. To the best of my knowledge, no account of the contrast between *connaître* and regular Vs like e.g. *choisir* exists in any framework, nor does any proposal exist as to the reason

I would like to thank Judith Aissen, Probal Dasgupta, Carol Rosen, Nicolas Ruwet, and Liliane Tasmowski for many helpful criticisms of earlier versions of this study. Special appreciation is due to Marie-Madeleine Saphire for her many hours of patient consulting about the French data and for checking all of the judgments recorded here. No one but the author is, however, responsible for any errors or shortcomings.

why a few Vs like *connaître* appear to violate the constraint blocking *(Ab). A priori, it is, of course, possible that the behavior of Vs like *connaître* in (B) is just an insignificant irregularity, of no more import than, e.g., the fact that the plural form of the English noun *mouse* is *mice* instead of what would be the regular *mouses*.

However, this study argues, to the contrary, that the behavior of French Vs like *connaître* is a phenomenon entirely distinct in nature from that of the plural of *mouse*. It is indicated that the apparently irregular distribution in (B) is actually a symptom of a deeper regularity, a straightforward consequence of the fact that the complement clauses in (B) contrast in a nonobvious way with those in (A). The arguments for this conclusion depend on documenting that complements like that of (B) contrast with those of (A) in other ways beyond appearing not to obey the constraint in *(Ab).

It is shown how, internal to a body of assumptions about clause structures in general and the kind of causative sentences represented by (A) and (B) in particular, the apparent irregularities and special features of complement Vs like *connaître* can all be reduced to a single basic fact: such Vs can occur in certain clause types just in case these are complements of *faire*. More precisely, despite the obvious superficial parallelism between (A) and (B), it is argued that while the complement of (A) is, as in effect traditionally assumed, a standard transitive clause, that of the apparently irregular (Bb) is actually what is called in relational grammar work an INVERSION clause, that is, one in which a subject is demoted to indirect object.

If the conclusions just previewed are correct, various consequences of relevance to grammatical theory follow. Internal to relational frameworks, a number of distinct assumptions are shown to be either supported or rendered untenable. External to such frameworks, the results of this work are argued to bear on the now revived question of whether the syntactic structure of a sentence can be identified with its superficial form. If anything like the overall argument of this work is valid, no such identification is viable. Finally, it turns out that the basic analysis of French supported in this inquiry is incompatible with certain fundamental views of the 'government-binding' version of transformational grammar. Consequently, the present study points to the incorrectness of those assumptions.

So, while the investigation which follows is basically a descriptive analysis of French, its real import lies in its implications for the formulation of viable grammatical theories. My hope is that through a extensively worked out analysis of a highly constrained domain, the account which follows provides a test case of the sort of (correct) analyses of NL fragments which an adequate grammatical theory should make available and with which it cannot be permitted to be incompatible.

Abbreviations

A⟨b⟩	An arc A whose tail node is b
APG	Arc Pair Grammar
⟨b⟩	Node b
$c_{final}\langle b\rangle$	The final stratum of node b
CIC	Cohesive Infinitive Construction
$c_{initial}\langle b\rangle$	The initial stratum of node b
$c_k\langle b\rangle$	The c_kth stratum of node b
C(lause)⟨b⟩	A clause whose highest (defining) node is b
CU	Clause Union
CU-image	Clause Union image
EXI	Extraposition of Indefinite Construction
FC	Fancy Constraint
FCOP	Fancy Constraint Override Phenomenon
hir	Him or Her
MA	Manner Adverbial
NL	Natural Language
1AEX	1 Advancement Exclusiveness Law
P	Predicate
PC	Pronominal Clitic
PN	Pair Network
P-Phrase	Purposive Phrase
RFX1	Reflexive/Reciprocal 1 Restriction
RG	Relational Grammar
RPPO	Reflexive Passive Person Override
R-sign	Relational Sign
S-graph	Surface Graph
S-Phrase	*Sans* Phrase
U	Union
V	Verb

Introduction

Examples (1) and (2) illustrate the much-discussed French causative or *faire* construction, which I refer to as the COHESIVE INFINITIVE CONSTRUCTION (CIC).[1]

(1) a. Le gardien a fait sortir les prisonniers.
"The guard made the prisoners go out."
b. On fera discuter Marie de cela.
"One/we will have Mary discuss that."
c. Cela fait rire tout le monde.
"That makes everybody laugh."

(2) a. Marcel a fait épouser sa fille au medecin.
"Marcel made the doctor marry his daughter."
b. On a fait choisir Martin et Claude à Jacques.
"One/we made Jacques choose Martin and Claude."
c. Cette vedette pourra faire oublier sa femme à ton collègue.
"That (film) star could make your colleague forget his wife."

The CIC appears to consist of a main clause with an embedded complement whose main V is an infinitive. The embedded V can be either intransitive, as in (1), or transitive, as in (2).

A characteristic property of the CIC is that what seems to be the maximally superficial subject (henceforth 1) of the complement appears to the right of the complement V.[2] There are several possibilities for the status of this complement 1 in the main clause. If the complement corresponds to an intransitive clause, its 1 normally appears as a 2 of the main clause, as in (1a,b,c), whose complements correspond, respectively, to the independent clauses in (3a,b,c).[3]

(3) a. Les prisonniers sont sortis.
"The prisoners went out."
b. Marie discutera de cela.
"Marie will discuss that."
c. Tout le monde rit.
"Everybody laughs."

When the complement is a transitive clause, as in (2), its superficial 1 is typically manifest as a 3 of the main clause, that is, as a phrase marked with the preposition *à* or its variants.[4] The complements in examples like (2) correspond to full transitive clauses of the respective forms in (4).[5]

(4) a. Le medecin a épousé sa fille.
"The doctor married his daughter."
b. Jacques a choisi Martin et Claude.
"Jacques chose Martin and Claude."
c. Ton collègue oubliera sa femme.
"Your colleague will forget his wife."

Consider analogues of (4) in which the 2 is PRONOMINAL. Notably, such a 2 cannot appear as a full personal pronoun; see Kayne (1975: chapter 2).

(5) a. *Le medecin a épousé elle.
"The doctor married her."
b. *Jacques a choisi eux.
"Jacques chose them."
c. *Ton collègue oubliera elle.
"Your colleague will forget her."
d. Le medecin l'a épousé.
"The doctor married him."
e. Jacques les a choisis.
"Jacques chose them."
f. Ton collègue l'oubliera.
"Your colleague forgot it/hir."[6]

Rather, in such sentences the 2 must be represented by one of the accusative pronominal clitics (PCs), appearing on the V, in a regular fashion, as in (5d,e,f).[7] There are CIC sentences whose complements correspond to (5):

(6) a. Marcel l'a fait épouser au medecin.
"Marcel made the doctor marry hir."
b. On les a fait choisir à Jacques.
"One/we had Jacques choose them."
c. Cette vedette pourra la faire oublier à ton collègue.
"That (film) star could make your colleague forget her."

Quite regularly, each such CIC structure contains an accusative PC representing the 2 of the embedding, this PC appearing on the CIC main V or its highest auxiliary.[8]

However, there is a notable gap in the class of CIC sentences analogous to (6) corresponding to cases where the embedded 2 is either NON-THIRD PERSON or anaphorically related to the main clause 1. Without this restriction, one would expect forms like (7) to be well-formed:

(7) a. *Marcel vous a fait épouser au medecin.
"Marcel had the doctor marry you."
b. *On nous a fait choisir à Jacques.
"One had Jacques choose us."

c. *Cette vedette se fera oublier à ton collègue.
"That (film) star$_i$ will make your colleague forget herself$_i$."

But examples of this type are systematically sharply ill-formed.[9] Let us refer to a nominal which is third person but NOT reflexive as PLAIN and to others as FANCY. Of course, what it means for a nominal to be reflexive is a complex issue and one beyond the bounds of this work; see Postal (to appear b). Informally and roughly, it suffices to think of a reflexive nominal for current purposes as one anaphorically connected to a 'local' antecedent, and it is sufficient to think of 'local' as meaning 'in the same clause'. See the discussion of (60a,b) below. Assuming that French PCs correspond to nominals,[10] one can then initially characterize the constraint visible in (7) by saying that a main clause CIC nominal corresponding to an embedded 2 cannot be fancy, that is, must be plain.[11] Henceforth this restriction is referred to as the FANCY CONSTRAINT (FC).[12]

The situation related to FC is more complicated than the discussion so far reveals. Even with the same main and embedded Vs as previously cited, the apparent downstairs superficial 2 of a CIC clause CAN be fancy if, instead of manifesting as a main clause 3, the apparent downstairs 1 appears as the object of the preposition *par* or, in limited cases, *de,* or does not appear at all. This is shown by the entirely grammatical examples in (8):

(8) a. Marcel vous a fait épouser par le medecin.
"Marcel had the doctor marry you."
b. On nous a fait choisir par Jacques.
"One had us chosen by Jacques."
c. Cette vedette se fera oublier par ton collègue.
"That (film) star will get/have herself forgotten by your colleague."
c. Cet adolescent s'est fait détester de tout le monde.
"That adolescent made himself be/got detested by everybody."
e. On nous a fait choisir.[13]
"One had us chosen."
f. Cet adolescent s'est fait détester.
"That adolescent made himself be/got detested."

So FC determines a gap in the class of CIC sentences whose complements are transitive clauses with a 2 which would determine a fancy main clause 2; but FC only holds when the complement 1 appears as a main clause 3. It does not hold when the complement shares features with nonreflexive personal passive clauses, as in (8), where the relevant nominals are marked just like the earlier 1s in French nonreflexive passives. Compare the independent nonreflexive personal passives in (9):

(9) a. Vous avez été épousée par le medecin.
"You have been married by the doctor."
b. Nous avons été choisis par Jacques.
"We have been chosen by Jacques."

c. Cette vedette sera oubliée par ton collègue.
"That (film) star will be forgotten by your colleague."
d. Cet adolescent est détesté de tout le monde.
"That adolescent is detested by everybody."
e. Nous avons été choisis.
"We have been chosen."
f. Cet adolescent est détesté.
"That adolescent is detested."

One goal of this study is to provide an account of FC which has the basic difference between *(7) and (8) as a consequence.

Despite what has been said so far, there exist certain well-known apparent exceptions to FC quite independent of structures like (8). These are CIC sentences where, even though the apparent superficial 1 of the complement manifests as a main clause 3, the lower 2 can nonetheless show up as a fancy main clause 2. The collection of complement Vs which permit this is extremely small, a fact argued in chapter 6 to be devoid of significance. While membership for particular speakers may vary somewhat, I have found no clear cases for my consultants beyond *connaître* 'to know', *reconnaître* 'to recognize', and *voir* 'to see'. These are, moreover, the Vs cited in the literature as appearing in such contexts; see Sanfeld (1965: 182–85), Kayne (1975: 298n), Morin (1977: 21), Hendrick (1978: 240–41), Tasmowski-de Ryck (1985: 259, 308).

(10) a. On vous fera connaître à Louise.
"One/we will have Louise know (meet) you."
b. Le président s'est fait reconnaître à Louise.
"The $president_i$ had Louise recognize $himself_i$."
c. Jacques nous a fait voir à ses chefs.
"Jacques had his bosses see us."
d. André doit se faire connaître à l'agent de liaison.
"Andre must make himself known to the liaison agent."

The existence of sentences like (10) represents an odd circumstance. In terms of the basic CIC pattern with transitive embeddings, (10a–e) appear perfectly regular. Yet with respect to the normal FC gap, they are exceptional. So examples (10a–e) seem to constitute a grammatical peculiarity: an exceptional regularity.

How should a grammar of French account for (10a–e)? An obvious answer would be that the formulation of FC, in no matter what terms turn out to be appropriate, should just reference the embedded V and limit the constraint on fancy 2s to Vs other than the handful of exceptions. There is no evident a priori reason why such a treatment could not be right. But one descriptive goal of this study is to argue that it is in fact incorrect. Rather, it is claimed that FC is entirely general and references no lexical items at all, either directly or indirectly; see (56) below. There is nonetheless a truly exceptional feature manifested in (10). But it will be argued that this lies in the structures of the embedded clauses, which are not what they seem. This partially exceptional structure only makes it appear that (10a–d) are exceptions to a thoroughly general statement of FC. By arguing for the analysis just hinted at, I will be able to lend support to a theoretical framework which makes available rather abstract relational representations of NL sentences.

One

Partially Correlated Anomalies

1.1 Some Apparently Odd Reflexive/Reciprocal Sentences

Consider (11a,b):

(11) a. *On vous fera critiquer/choisir/oublier à André.
"One/we will make Andre criticize/choose/forget you."
b. On vous fera connaître à André.
"One/we will make Andre know (meet) you."

Such contrasts reveal the difference between an ordinary transitive V and one of the Vs exceptional with respect to FC behavior. Let us call (transitive) Vs like those in (11a) STANDARD Vs and those like *connaître* in (10) and (11b) NONSTANDARD. Similarly, I will refer to examples like (10) as NONSTANDARD (CIC) SENTENCES and to those like (1) and (2) as STANDARD (CIC) SENTENCES.

One reason to suspect that the difference between standard and nonstandard Vs is NOT simply due to the fact that FC excludes the latter from its scope is revealed by the contrasts in (12) and (13):

(12) a. *La psychiatrie a fait critiquer/choisir/oublier Marcel à lui-même.
"Psychiatry made Marcel criticize/choose/forget himself."
b. La psychiatrie a fait connaître Marcel à lui-même.
"Psychiatry made Marcel know himself."

(13) a. *Cela fera critiquer/choisir/oublier ces gens l'un à l'autre.
"That will make these people criticize/choose/forget each other."
b. Cela fera connaître ces gens l'un à l'autre.
"That will make these people know each other."

While *(12a) and *(13a) are entirely impossible, (12b) and (13b) are essentially normal grammatical sentences.[1] This illustrates a regular distinction between standard Vs and *connaître*. Yet this contrast, which correlates with that in (11), is obviously not subsumable under FC itself. The latter refers to the status of a CIC main clause 2 as fancy, while the main clause 2s in (12) are both plain and, moreover, identical; and the same observation holds for (13). So the correlation between (10) on the one hand and (12b) and (13b) on the other cannot be reduced to FC and would remain an unaccounted-for accident if FC itself incorporated a clause excluding nonstandard Vs from its domain. One potential problem with this conclusion follows from the fact that sentences analogous to (12) and (13) can only be formed with the nonstandard V *connaître,* an issue discussed in section 3.4.

But the argument that facts like those illustrated in (11) do not reveal an idiosyncratic property of FC with respect to nonstandard Vs is greatly strengthened by the following observation. Although the CIC is found with several different main Vs, including *faire* 'to have (do), cause', *laisser* 'to let', and *voir* 'to see', nonstandard sentences like (10) are only possible with main V *faire.* While this might be attributed to semantic factors in the case of a main V like *voir,* no such appeal is possible with *laisser.* Yet the analogues of (10) with the latter main V are ungrammatical.

(14) a. *On vous laissera connaître à Louise.
"One/we will let Louise know (meet) you."
b. *Jacques nous a laissé voir à ces chefs.
"Jacques let his bosses see us."
c. *André doit se laisser connaître à l'agent de liaison.
"Andre$_i$ must let the liaison agent know (meet) himself$_i$."

These are ill-formed, although each represents a perfectly normal semantic structure. So apparent exceptions to FC are grammatically limited not only to nonstandard embedded Vs but to the single main V *faire.* Notably then, the same restriction holds for sentences like (12b) and (13b), whose analogues with *laisser* are also ungrammatical:

(15) a. *La psychiatrie a laissé connaître Marcel à lui-même.
"Psychiatry let Marcel know himself."
b. *Cela a laissé connaître ces gens l'un à l'autre.
"That let these people know each other."

The correlation between *(14) and *(15) argues that whatever principles allow nonstandard *connaître* to yield apparent exceptions to FC are the SAME as those which allow it, but not standard Vs, to appear as the complement V in (12b) and (13b). Because both nonstandard CIC phenomena are limited to the complements of *faire.* Since the properties of (12b) and (13b) cannot be reduced to exceptional mention of nonstandard Vs in FC itself, it follows that the phenomena under discussion have a basis distinct from lexical exclusions from the scope of FC.

The embedded propositions expressed by *(12a) and *(13a) would correspond to the independent clauses in (16):

(16) a. Marcel s'est critiqué/choisi/oublié.
"Marcel criticized/chose/forgot himself."
b. Ces gens se sont critiqués/choisis/oubliés (l'un l'autre).
"These people criticized/chose/forgot each other."

These each contain an accusative reflexive PC *se*. The way to express the meanings of *(12a) and *(13a) grammatically is to embed analogues of (16a,b), yielding regularly (17a,b), respectively:

(17) a. La psychiatrie a fait se critiquer/choisir/oublier Marcel.
"Psychiatry made Marcel criticize/choose/forget himself."
b. Cela a fait se critiquer/choisir/oublier ces gens (l'un l'autre).
"That made these people criticize/choose/forget each other."

These are easily seen to be consistent with FC, since it is the complement 1 which ends up as the main clause 2, while no complement 2 has any realization in the main clause.[2] Significantly, despite the existence of (12b) and (13b), sentences analogous to (17) are also possible with the nonstandard V *connaître:*

(18) a. La psychiatrie a fait se connaître Marcel.
"Psychiatry made Marcel know himself."
b. Cela a fait se connaître ces gens (l'un l'autre).
"That made these people know each other."

In short, in reflexive/reciprocal cases, *connaître* behaves as BOTH a standard and a nonstandard V. Section 4.1 considers the import of the ability of *connaître* and *voir* to behave in some respects as standard CIC Vs.

The facts about reflexives/reciprocals considered so far can be summed up as follows: when a CIC embedding corresponds to a clause containing anaphorically linked 1 and 2, only a nonstandard V permits a result in which (1) there is no reflexive PC, (2) the apparent embedded final 2 appears as main clause 2, and (3) the apparent embedded final 1 appears as a main clause 3 of the regular disjunctive reflexive form ⟨à Pronoun + même⟩ or the regular disjunctive reciprocal form ⟨l'un à l'autre/les uns aux autres⟩; moreover, these features are only possible in the complements of *faire*. A proper account of nonstandard V structures must then not only provide a basis for these properties but also for their partial correlation with FC.

1.2 Further Odd Reflexive Sentences

A second ground, related to that developed in section 1.1, also argues against a formulation of FC that references nonstandard Vs. When the 2 and 3 of a simple French clause are 'coreferents', the normal situation is for the 2 to antecede a disjunctive reflexive pronominal 3 of the form *à Pronoun + même*. But the 'reverse' situation, with the 3 anteceding a disjunctive pronominal 2 of the form *Pronoun + même* is, although less acceptable, for some speakers by no means impossible:

(19) a. J'ai décrit cet aveugle à lui-même.
b. ?J'ai décrit lui-même à cet aveugle.
"I described that blind man to himself."

Notably, the judgments in (19) appear to correlate with those in (20):

(20) a. *La psychiatrie a fait critiquer/choisir/oublier lui-même à cet aveugle.
"Psychiatry made that blind man criticize/choose/forget himself."

b. ?La psychiatrie a fait connaître lui-même à cet aveugle.
"Psychiatry made that blind man know himself."

Again, standard Vs contrast with *connaître* in a way not naturally reducible to FC itself.[3] Once more though, the situation is clouded by the fact that the nonstandard Vs *reconnaître* and *voir* also do not permit analogues of (20b); see section 3.4. However, as with *(14) and *(15), the argument is strengthened by the fact that the relatively weak possibility in (20b) is also exclusively limited to the complement of *faire:*

(21) *La psychiatrie a laissé connaître lui-même à cet aveugle.
"Psychiatry let that blind man know himself."

Despite the marginal character of (20b), it is nonetheless judged in a way which contrasts with *(21). This is another property which correlates with the distribution of FC.[4]

Moreover, the correlation between (19b) and (20b) can be strengthened, and in a way which supports the view that both are well-formed. The fact is that for my consultant, analogues of (19b) are only possible with THIRD PERSON nominals. Hence (22a,b) contrast sharply with (19b):

(22) a. *On a décrit vous-mêmes à vous et à votre frère.
"One/we described yourselves to you and your brother."

b. *On a décrit nous-mêmes à l'autre aveugle et à moi.
"One described ourselves to the other blind person and me."

But if *(22a,b) contrast with (19b), the latter is arguably well-formed. Moreover, the reality of the contrast between *(22a,b) and (19b) is shown by the fact that it is preserved in the passivelike construction with *se faire:*

(23) a. L'aveugle s'est fait décrire lui-même (par l'infirmière).
"The blind man got described to himself (by the nurse)."

b. *Vous et votre frère se feront décrire vous-mêmes (par l'infirmière).
"You and your brother will get described to yourselves (by the nurse)."

The key point is that parallels to (20b) are equally impossible with non–third person nominals:

(24) a. *La psychiatrie a fait connaître vous-mêmes à vous et à votre frère.
"Psychiatry made you and your brother know yourselves."

b. *La psychiatrie a fait connaître nous-mêmes à l'autre aveugle et à moi.
"Psychiatry made the other blind person and me know ourselves."

Thus it seems clear that the principles which allow sentences like (20b) with nonstandard Vs are intimately related to the principles permitting sentences like (19b) and (23a). This fact can in no way be reduced to exceptional mentioning of nonstandard Vs in some formulation of FC.

1.3 A Constraint on Reflexive/Reciprocal 1s

Now return to (12b) and (13b), repeated as (25):

(25) a. La psychiatrie a fait connaître Marcel à lui-même.
"Psychiatry made Marcel know himself."
b. Cela fera connaître ces gens l'un à l'autre.
"That will make these people know each other."

As already indicated, such examples are exceptional in a way not reducible to FC, because of the plain character of their main clause 2s. This is a second anomaly of the nonstandard V *connaître* beyond its apparent failure to be governed by FC (when embedded below *faire*). A third anomaly associated with this V is the possibility in (20b). Another key feature of (25) amounts to a fourth anomaly apparently manifested by *connaître*.

Assume, as I have implicitly done so far, that (25a,b) just involve CIC complements which are standard transitive clauses with, in each case, the main clause 3 corresponding to the superficial 1 of that clause, and the main clause 2 to its superficial 2.[5] Then underlying (25a,b) must be respective embedded complement clauses of the forms in (26), that is, with a superficial reflexive or reciprocal 1 anteceded by the superficial 2 (matching subscripts on nominals here and below indicate anaphoric linkages).

(26) a. ⟨lui-même$_i$ connaître Marcel$_i$⟩
b. ⟨l'un l'autre$_i$ connaître ces gens$_i$⟩

But an otherwise exceptionless French regularity precludes the superficial 1 of a clause being a reflexive or reciprocal form anaphorically related to another nominal in that clause:

(27) a. *Lui-même$_i$ connaît Marcel$_i$.
"Himself knows Marcel."
b. *Vous-mêmes$_i$ devrez répondre à vous et à votre frère$_i$.
"Yourselves should reply to you and your brother."
c. *Elle-même$_i$ déteste Lucille$_i$.
"Herself detests Lucille."
d. *Elle-même$_i$ est détesté de Lucille$_i$.
"Herself is detested by Lucille."
e. *Moi-même a/ai été décrit à Lucille par moi.
"Myself has been described to Lucille by me."
f. *Lui-même$_i$ a voté pour l'ancien maire$_i$.
"Himself voted for the former mayor."

(28) a. Ces gens$_i$ se critiqueront l'un l'autre$_i$.
"These people will criticize each other."
b. *L'un l'autre$_i$ (se) critiqueront ces gens$_i$.
"Each other will criticize these people."
c. *L'un l'autre$_i$ seront critiqués par ces gens$_i$.
"Each other will be criticized by these people."

d. *L'un l'autre$_i$ ont été décrits à ces gens$_i$.
"Each other were described to these people."

This constraint, call it the REFLEXIVE/RECIPROCAL 1 RESTRICTION (RFX1), manifests itself even in sentences related to (19b), as shown in (29):

(29) a. ?On a décrit lui-même$_i$ à cet aveugle$_i$.
"One/we described himself to that blind man."
b. *Lui-même$_i$ a été décrit à cet aveugle$_i$.
"Himself was described to that blind man."
c. *Lui-même$_i$ s'est fait décrire à cet aveugle$_i$.
"Himself had himself/got described to that blind man."
d. *A cet aveugle$_i$, lui-même$_i$ a été décrit.
"To that blind man, himself was described."
e. *Cet aveugle$_i$, lui-même$_i$ lui$_i$ a été décrit.
"That blind man, himself was described to himself."

The contrast between (29a) and *(29b,c) shows that RFX1 is not a mere linear precedence condition between antecedent and reflexive/reciprocal pronoun. This conclusion is reinforced by *(29d,e), in which such a condition holds without eliminating the violation.

Note that the problem involving RFX1 and the CIC can only arise for a nonstandard V, because *(20a) illustrates that the key CIC sentences are impossible with standard Vs. In fact, only *connaître* seems to allow such sentences. Thus, given the usual assumptions, under which the apparent exceptions to FC involve standard transitive embeddings, one must allow embedding a clause as a CIC complement to somehow rescue that clause from RFX1, complicating the statement of that restriction. In the absence of cases like (25a,b), RFX1 could be stated informally as in (30):[6]

(30) RFX1
The superficial 1 of clause C cannot be a reflexive/reciprocal pronoun anaphorically related to another nominal constituent of C.

The complication is that for reasons involving only examples like (25), RFX1 is not statable as in (30) or its equivalents but must reference more global structures in which clauses containing superficial reflexive/reciprocal 1s are embedded.[7] This fourth anomaly, again linked exclusively to nonstandard Vs, suggests that structures which appear to be exceptions to FC actually involve some grammatical features not incorporable as a list of exceptions in the formulation of FC itself.

1.4 Implications of the Correlated Anomalies

Enough has been said to suggest strongly that a standard approach to nonstandard Vs cannot be adequate. That nonstandard Vs are apparent exceptions to FC is not a fact in itself but a symptom of some as yet obscure property which renders the nonstandard CIC complements special in other ways as well. The problem then is to find a less obvious but relatively unified treatment which can eliminate the various anomalies. More precisely, one needs to show that nonstandard complements have certain nonapparent structural features, and that given these, the apparent anomalies documented so far and others to be attested below vanish. In other words, one needs to formulate and justify an account in which the complements of nonstandard CIC sentences contrast structurally with those of standard CIC sentences, in spite of their superficial similarities. Development of such a treatment requires a sketch of what I consider the correct overall relational description of the CIC. This account takes this construction to be a special case of a universally characterizable class of forms called CLAUSE UNION structures.

Two

The CIC as a Clause Union Structure

2.1 Fragments of the Arc Pair Grammar Framework

The hypotheses about French central to this study are formulated, in general informally, in terms of the Arc Pair Grammar (APG) framework developed and discussed in Johnson and Postal (1980), Postal (1982, 1985, 1986a, 1986b, to appear a, to appear b); see also Aissen (1987, to appear). It is thus necessary to sketch certain aspects of this approach, which is in many respects a development of ideas in Relational Grammar (RG); see Perlmutter (1983), Perlmutter and Rosen (1984), and references in Dubinsky and Rosen (1987).

In APG terms, an NL sentence is analyzed as an object called a PAIR NETWORK (PN). Each PN consists of two primitive binary relations between objects called ARCS; the latter are fundamentally the same as those of RG representations. The relations between arcs are named SPONSOR and ERASE. That is, a PN is a collection of ordered pairs of arcs. Arcs are based on three types of primitives: NODES, which represent grammatical elements of all sorts, R(ELATIONAL)-SIGNS, which are the names of (primitive) grammatical relations between elements, and COORDINATES, which define linguistic levels for fixed elements. R-signs relevant for this discussion include those in (31):

(31) Primitive Grammatical Relation — Name = R-sign

Primitive Grammatical Relation	Name = R-sign
NOMINAL RELATIONS	
Subject	1
Direct Object	2
Indirect Object	3
Demiobject	4
Semiobject	5
Quasiobject	6
Chômeur	8
Dead	9

VERBAL RELATIONS

Predicate	P
Union	U

The relations in this subset hold between various types of constituents and the elements defining clauses. They are thus aspects of clause syntax. Some of the relations in (31) are in effect traditional, while others are not. Nontraditional relations are central to the APG analysis of a wide range of NL clause phenomena. The interpretation of arcs is given in (32).

(32) 100

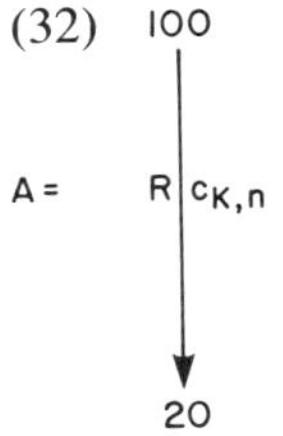

A = R | $c_{K,n}$ Node 20 (= A's HEAD) bears the relation named by R to node 100 (= A's TAIL) at all the levels k to n of node 100.

20

For example, if R = 3, then (32) says that node 20 is an indirect object of node 100 at all the levels k to n of node 100. In what follows, I make use of notations like '⟨b⟩', 'A⟨b⟩', 'C(lause)⟨b⟩', and 'c_k⟨b⟩' to refer, respectively, to node b, an arc A whose tail is node b, a clause defined by node b, and the c_kth stratum of node b; see below for a definition of 'stratum'.

Sponsor and Erase are primitives. To say that one arc A sponsors another B is to say that A 'is a creator of' B or, less metaphorically, that A is a necessary condition for the existence of B. So recognition of the Sponsor relation involves the claim that some grammatical relations in a sentence depend on the existence of others. Each arc has at least one sponsor and no more than two; some arcs sponsor themselves. The latter and only these have the coordinate c_1; these are called INITIAL arcs. Since all and only initial arcs sponsor themselves, one can, as in all following PN representations, suppress the marking of self-sponsorship. To say that A erases B is to say that B represents a grammatical relation borne by B's head node, which is, however, NOT a surface relation. Moreover, this nonsurface status is due to the existence of A. Thus the overall SURFACE form of a PN, Q, consists of all and only those arcs in Q which are NOT erased.

To illustrate these ideas initially, consider the French example in (33a), an instance of the Extraposition of Indefinite (EXI) construction. In most cases, this exists as an alternative to standard examples like (33b).

(33) a. Il arrivera un paquet.
b. Un paquet arrivera.
"A package will arrive."

Thus, in an EXI construction, a nominal which would otherwise appear, as in (33b), as a final 1, appears postverbally, while a dummy nominal, more precisely a nominative PC *il* representing a dummy nominal, is present. Henceforth postverbal nominals like *un paquet* in (33a) will be referred to as EXI PIVOTS. Under the analysis suggested in Postal (1986a: chapter 5), an EXI sentence like (33a) would have a partial PN structure like (34).

(34)

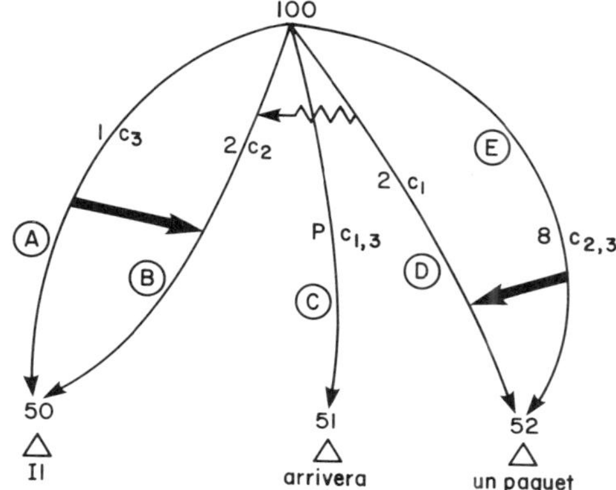

The representation in (34) makes use of the notational conventions in (35) for diagrammatically representing Sponsor, Erase, and one of their frequent combinations in PN representations.

(35)

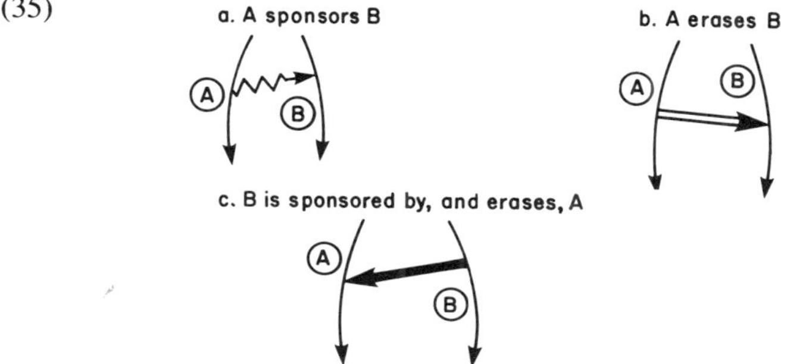

The clause represented in (34) involves five arcs, A, B, C, D, E, each having the tail node 100. Arcs with the same tail node are called NEIGHBORS. So A, B, C, D, and E in (34) are neighbors. The head nodes of these arcs, 50, 51, and 52, represent the distinct constituents of the clause designated 100.

There are more neighbors with tail 100 in (34) than there are constituents, because an individual element can bear more than one relation to a fixed element. These relations are, however, stratified into levels or STRATA. A stratum can be taken as a maximal set of neighbors sharing a fixed coordinate. Thus (34) defines the three strata for node 100 listed in (36):

(36) a. The 1st = {C,D}
b. The 2nd = {B,C,E}
c. The 3rd = {A,C,E}

The 1st stratum, containing the only initial (self-sponsoring) arcs, defines (33a) as a so-called UNACCUSATIVE structure (see below), that is, an intransitive clause with an initial 2-arc but no initial 1-arc. The 3rd stratum is the final stratum. Although (34) contains a 1-arc and a 2-arc, in fact, two different 2-arcs, there is a clear sense in which it is NOT a transitive structure. For no SINGLE stratum contains both a 1-arc and a 2-arc. Rather, PN (34) claims that while the EXI pivot *un paquet* is an initial 2 of the clause, it is a final 8, as argued in Postal (1986a: chapter 5; 1986b). In such a framework, it is of course potentially equivocal to ask questions like 'Is such and such constituent a 1?', unless one specifies levels. For a given constituent can be a 1 in one stratum of a fixed node but not a 1 in another stratum of that node.

The left-to-right orientation of arcs in PN representations like (34) is strictly meaningless and does not necessarily correspond to any feature of PNs; it does not formally represent word order or any other linguistic reality. It is suggested in Postal (1986a: 20–21) that linear order can be represented in PNs by the choice of nonterminal nodes like 50, 51, etc., with left-to-right order corresponding to the arithmetical Less Than relation among these nodes. Under this interpretation, (34) is a significantly different structure from one in which e.g. nodes 51 and 52 are interchanged, since the latter would correspond to a non-French string like (37):[1]

(37) *Il un paquet arrivera.
"A package will arrive."

Sponsor and Erase permit the 'extraction' from each PN of certain substructures definable as sets of arcs. One such substructure consists of the set of all self-sponsoring arcs; in (34), this is the set consisting of C and D. The system of Johnson and Postal (1980) claimed that only these arcs could be semantically relevant. Another designated collection consists of the set of all arcs which are NOT erased. The latter defines a representation roughly equivalent to the surface structures of other approaches. In (34) this set of arcs, referred to as the S(URFACE)-GRAPH of the PN, contains only A, C, and E. The word order definition in terms of arithmetical properties of nodes mentioned above is relevant only for those nodes which are the heads of surface (unerased) arcs, under the assumption, which I take to be correct, that only surface forms have a linear order specified. Thus, the word order of (33a) is determined exclusively over the heads of the surface arcs A, C, and E. Arcs B and D are irrelevant for word order.

If arcs A and B are distinct, have the same head node—that is, OVERLAP—and A sponsors B, then A is a PREDECESSOR of B, and B conversely a SUCCESSOR of A. So in (34), A is a successor of B and E a successor of D. That all the predecessors in (34) are erased was taken to be determined by law in Johnson and Postal (1980); in that system, ALL predecessors are erased. More recent work suggests that there is a limited class of unerased predecessors; see Aissen (1987) and Postal (to appear b). But this is irrelevant for the present discussion, and one can safely assume that all predecessors in the domain under discussion are erased. If so, predecessors are irrelevant to word order determination.

APG successors define phenomena of the sort which in transformational grammar motivate the notion of movement. The Successor/Predecessor relation provides an analysis of various distinct primitive relations borne by individual constituents into chains, with the ultimate predecessor the first member of the chain and the ultimate successor the final member. Successors divide into two fundamental classes, depending on whether the predecessor/successor pair are neighbors. If they are, the relations are LOCAL, if not FOREIGN. So in (34), E is a local successor of D, and A a local successor of B. Local successor relations correspond in general to the Revaluations (Advancements and Demotions) of RG. Foreign successor relations reconstruct, in particular, various 'raising' phenomena.

Assume that one can define a class of structures called (BASIC) CLAUSE STRUCTURES; see Johnson and Postal (1980: chapter 7). Each consists of a self-sponsoring P-arc and at least one self-sponsoring NUCLEAR TERM (1 or 2) arc, plus optionally other arcs. Basic clauses are the minimal kinds of clauses. The representation in (34) is a basic clause structure. The heads of self-sponsoring P-arcs correspond roughly to verbal/adjectival elements, while the heads of Nominal (1, 2, 3, 4, 5, 6, 8, 9, etc.) arcs correspond to nominal constituents. It is possible that each full sentence of any NL contains at least one basic clause.

2.2 Fragments of a Theory of Clause Union Structures

Against the extremely sketchy background of section 2.1, one can consider the proper analysis of the CIC in APG terms. The claim is that the CIC is an instantiation of a type of basic clause structure referred to as CLAUSE UNION (CU) structures.[2] The key idea is that such structures are defined by a traditionally unrecognized grammatical relation called UNION (R-sign = U).[3] U is an additional relation beyond P which a verbal element can bear to a clause. More specifically, a CU structure exists when the predicate of a subordinate clause bears the relation U to the immediately containing main clause. Hence, formally, U-arcs are foreign successors, basically of P-arcs.[4] One can assume that the relevant subordinate clauses, at least for French, are always 2 complements, and thus that U is relevant to structures of the form in (38).

(38)

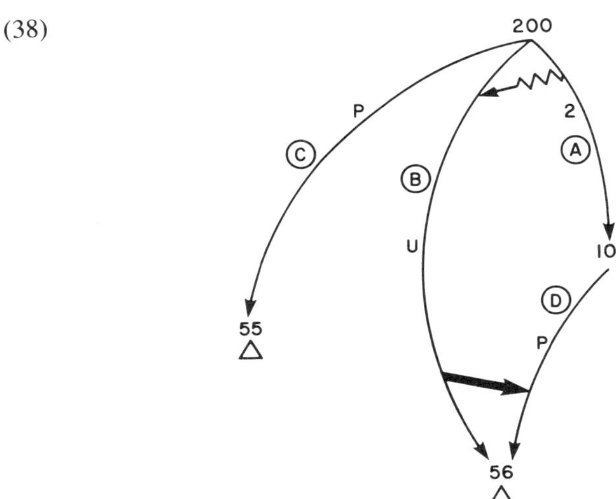

A substructure like (38) defines the clause 200 as a CU structure. That is, a CU structure is one in which a P-arc branch of a 2-arc like A has a U-arc foreign successor like B, which is a neighbor of A.[5] Such a construction inherently yields main clauses which are at least biverbal, in that they contain distinct neighboring verbal arcs, one a P-arc and one a U-arc.[6] So in a CU construction, the initial verbal element of a complement is a superficial constituent of the immediately dominating main clause. A CU construction is thus a special type of basic clause structure containing a subordinate basic clause whose constituents are noninitial constituents of the main clause.

A key aspect of CU structures concerns the nonverbal constituents of the complement. Roughly, those nonverbal constituents which would be surface constituents of the complement clause were it NOT embedded are also constituents of the main clause. This can be taken to mean that a relevant subset of the neighbors of the P-arc (like D in (34)) defining the CU structure (must) have foreign successors in the main clause. In other words, a CU structure can be more fully specified, as in (39).

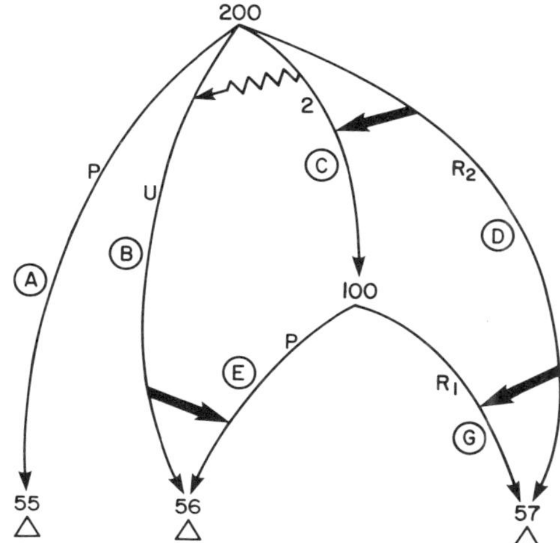

It is important to pick out exactly which arcs like G in CU complements such as that of (39) must be FORCED (by law) to have foreign successors in the main clause. Such arcs are called LAUNCHERS in Johnson and Postal (1980). An elegant specification of the class of launchers is possible; see Johnson and Postal (1980: chapter 8) and Postal (to appear b). Space precludes a discussion of this topic here. But one principle needs to be stressed. Every neighbor of the complement P-arc of a CU complement which has no eraser INTERNAL TO THE COMPLEMENT is a launcher. It follows that every arc having the CU complement defining node as tail node is erased, and hence a CU complement has no SURFACE existence. Thus CU structures involve underlying biclausal structures whose surface structures are monoclausal.

I refer to the (foreign) successor of a launcher as its C(LAUSE) U(NION))–IMAGE. So in (39), D is the CU-image of G. There is reason to believe that regularities statable in grammatical theory link the R-signs of CU-images to those of their launcher predecessors. These regularities determine, beyond the assignment of CU complement constituents to the main clause, (some of) the relations these constituents bear in the main clause. I assume that one such regularity is that every nominal arc launcher has a 9-arc CU-image. This view is novel here, not being found in previous RG or APG treatments, where, in particular, 1-arc and 2-arc launchers were NEVER taken to have 9-arc CU-images; the latter were limited at best to 3-arc, oblique-arc, etc., launchers. The wider distribution of 9-arc CU-images can, I believe, be justified, although the arguments are involved and abstract; see Postal (to appear b) and the discussion following (54) below. Here I simply assume this position, which is NOT crucial to the current discussion. That is, the essential results of this study would survive in a more traditional relational view of CU clauses or in that of e.g. Gibson and Raposo (1986). But given the current position, if G in (39) is a 1, 2, 3, 4, 5, 6, 8, 9, etc., arc, then D is a 9-arc.

The view that all nominal arc launchers have 9-arc CU-images in no way entails that CU complement nominal constituents NECESSARILY function as main clause SURFACE 9s. For CU-images can have local successors, referred to here as POSTIMAGES. A question is to what extent grammatical theory requires the existence of postimages in particular cases. My view is that grammatical law does not determine this to be necessary. But this is not relevant to the current discussion, since I assume that French grammar requires at least each Term (1, 2, 3) arc launcher to have a postimage (as well as a CU-image); see (42b).[7]

The regularity which holds of launchers—that they are not erased internal to CIC complements (that is, the arc which erases a launcher is external to the complement containing that launcher)—follows in effect from two principles. One, subsuming a previously noted generalization—that each predecessor is erased—is that each launcher is erased in particular by its CU-image. The other is a fundamental APG law which says that no arc has more than one eraser. Consequently, no local predecessor in a CIC complement can be a launcher. And it also turns out that only final-stratum arcs can be launchers.[8]

I suggest that significant regularities in the domain of CU constructions involve relations between launchers and their postimages, where A is the postimage of a launcher B if and only if A is the local successor of the CU-image of A. I limit attention to postimages of nominal arc launchers, which are then local successors of 9-arcs. The regularities in question cover the same domain treated by regularities between launchers and CU-images in different relational treatments not recognizing the current distinction between CU-image and lawfully constrained postimages, e.g. those of Johnson and Postal (1980: chapter 8), Gibson and Raposo (1986), and Davies and Rosen (1985). Specifically, I assume that the grammatical LAWS in (40) restrict the R-signs of the postimages of nominal arc launchers.

(40) Some Hypothesized Universal Postimage Constraints

Let R2 be the R-sign of a postimage of a NOMINAL arc launcher A whose R-sign is R1. Then:

(a) POSTIMAGE PRINCIPLE A

If A is not a 1-arc, then R2 = R1.[9]

(b) POSTIMAGE PRINCIPLE B1

If A is a 1-arc, then R2 = 2 or 3.

(c) POSTIMAGE PRINCIPLE B2

If A is a 1-arc local successor of an arc whose R-sign is R3, then R2 = R3.

These hypothesized laws are thus relevant to the determination of the R-signs of arcs like D in CU structures like (41).

(41)

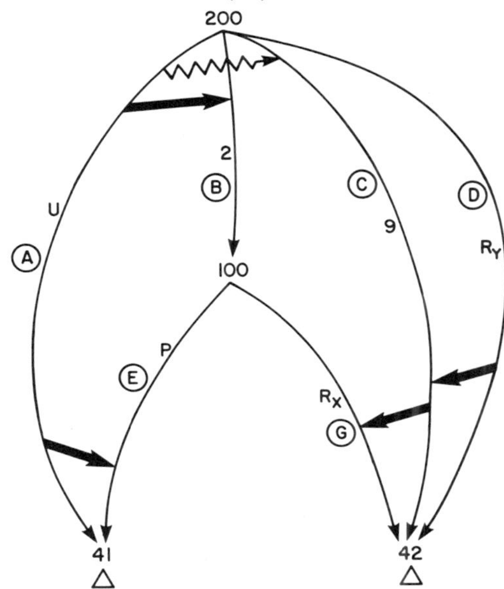

Limiting attention to Term arcs, consider what these proposed grammatical laws say. Suppose A is a 3-arc launcher. Then the theory states that A has a 9-arc CU-image and a 3-arc postimage (if any). Suppose A is a 2-arc launcher. Then the theory claims that A has a 9-arc CU-image and a 2-arc postimage (if any). Suppose A is a 1-arc. Then the theory specifies that A has a 9-arc CU-image, and if it has a postimage, the latter is either a 2- or a 3-arc. But if A is the local successor of a 2-arc, then the postimage is a 2-arc. If A is not a local successor, then the theory allows A to be either a 2- or a 3-arc, subject to still further grammatical laws and to NL-particular constraints.

One of the latter constraints apparently relevant for French is formulable roughly as in (42a):

(42) a. *French Postimage Principle 1*
If A is an initial 1-arc, then R2 = 3.[10]

b. *French Postimage Principle 2*
If A is a Term-arc launcher, then A has a postimage.

Principle (42a) limits the freedom permitted for non–local successor 1-arc launchers by Postimage Principle B1.[11] Principle (42b) imposes the constraint mentioned earlier, which requires (at least) all French Term-arc launchers to have postimages. It thus requires every Term-arc launcher to head some (local successor) term-arc in the main clause. If earlier RG ideas about CU constructions had been correct, then the effect of (42b) was guaranteed by grammatical laws. But more recent work casts doubt on this possibility. For example, Gerdts (to appear) discusses a class of 'no revaluation' causative sentences in Korean. She shows that these have properties of CU structures but are such that the complement 1 does not head a main clause term-arc. In present terms, these would be analyzed as cases where the 9-arc CU-image of the 1-arc has no postimage (although Gerdts's analysis is somewhat different). Notably, French has no analogues of the sentences Gerdts discusses, a state of affairs guaranteed by (42b).

One can illustrate the application of this account of CU structures to the CIC, under the assumption that the CIC IS a CU structure. A few informal remarks are in order, which can be based on CIC cases like (43):

(43) a. On a vu sortir les abeilles.
"One/we saw the bees go out."
b. Jacques fera danser sa femme.
"Jacques will have his wife dance."

First, rules not considered here must guarantee that the verbal element heading a French U-arc has infinitival form. Second, French word order rules must determine that surface Ps precede surface Us, which in turn precede surface nominal constituents other than 1s, including 2s like *les abeilles* in (43a) and *sa femme* in (43b). These matters need not concern us here.

Consider then CIC cases assumed to have complements which are simple transitive clauses such as that in (44a), which corresponds to the independent clause (44b).

(44) a. Louise fera manger des carottes aux enfants.
"Louise will have the children eat carrots."
b. Les enfants mangeront des carottes.
"The children will eat carrots."

As is well-known, in cases like (44a), the complement 2 appears as a main clause 2, and the complement 1 as main clause 3. This would follow directly from the principles in (40) and (42), assuming a structure for (44a) like (45). Note that this PN representation and all following ones ignore the structure associated with prepositional phrases and essentially treat sentences as if they contained no prepositions. This is not relevant to current goals.

(45)

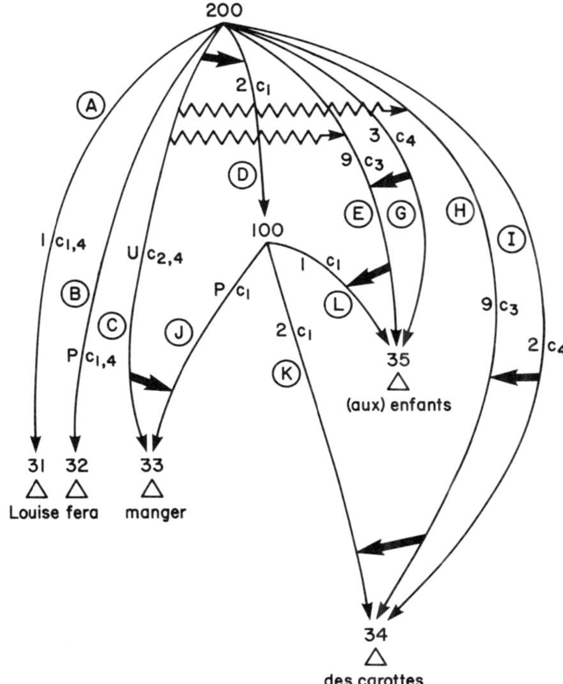

In this PN, K and L are nominal-arc launchers and thus have 9-arc CU-images; these are H and E, respectively. According to Postimage Principle A, K has a 2-arc postimage, I, and according to Postimage Principle B1, L has a postimage which is either a 2- or 3-arc. Since L is initial, French Postimage Principle 1 specifies further that the relevant postimage, G, must be a 3-arc, as it is.

Evidently standard diagrammatic representations of PNs for CU structures are quite unwieldy because of the complexity of even relatively simple CU clauses. Moreover, for current purposes, which focus on the relations between launchers and postimages, much of the structure is repetitive from PN to PN, and some of the rest is not relevant. It is thus useful to introduce a much simpler system of representation which focuses on launchers and their successors. I therefore utilize a 'box' notation, which yields (46) as a reduction of (45):

(46)

Louise	des carottes	(aux) enfants
1	2	3
1	9	9
1	—	—
1	—	—
═══	═══	═══
	2	1

In this notation, a double line separates the structure of the complement (below the double line) from that of the main clause. Each row corresponds to a stratum, and the entries in each column indicate the R-sign of the arc headed by the nominals at the top of that column in that stratum of the relevant clause. LOWER lines represent earlier strata than higher lines. Hence (46) indicates that the subordinate clause is a single-stratum structure, while the main clause has four strata. The complement constituents do not appear in the earliest two strata of the main clause. But each heads a 9-arc CU-image in the third stratum, and the relevant postimage in the fourth. The repeated main clause first and second strata give no real information; hence such identical patterns are hereafter compressed into a single row.

Consider next a CIC example like (47a), whose complement seems to correspond essentially to a personal passive clause like (47b).

(47) a. Louise a fait laver la voiture par Jacques.
"Louise had the car washed by Jacques."
b. La voiture a été lavée par Jacques.
"The car was washed by Jacques."

Assuming that the complement in (47a) IS a passive clause (a controversial assumption discussed and refined further in chapter 3), (47a) would have a PN yielding a box diagram like (48):

(48)

Louise	la voiture	(par) Jacques
1	2	8
1	9	9
1	—	—
═══	═══	═══
	1	8
	2	1

In this case, the launcher headed by *la voiture* has a 2-arc postimage as a consequence of Postimage Principle B2.

Next consider a CIC case like (49a), whose complement corresponds to the personal passive clause in (49b):

(49) a. Marthe fera présenter Jérôme à Louise par Théodore.
"Marthe will have Jerome introduced to Louise by Theodore."
b. Jérôme sera présenté à Louise par Théodore.
"Jerome will be introduced to Louise by Theodore."

Assuming again a personal passive analysis of the CIC complement, (49a) would correspond to a PN yielding a box diagram like (50):

(50)

Marthe	Jérôme	(à) Louise	(par) Théodore
1	2	3	8
1	9	9	9
1	—	—	—
	1	3	8
	2	3	1

Here Postimage Principle B2 determines that the 1-arc launcher headed by *Jérôme* has a 2-arc postimage, while Postimage Principle A determines that the 3-arc launcher headed by *Louise* has a 3-arc postimage.

Next take a CIC case where the complement corresponds to a putatively unaccusative intransitive clause:

(51) a. Marcel a fait tomber le verre.
"Marcel made the glass fall."
b. Le verre est tombé.
"The glass fell."

The relevant PN would determine a box diagram like (52):

(52)

Marcel	le verre
1	2
1	9
1	—
	1
	2

It is the assumption that (51a) is an unaccusative structure which determines the two-strata analysis of the complement. The fact that the postimage whose head is *le verre* is a 2-arc then follows from Postimage Principle B2.

Consider cases in which the complement is an active clause containing an initial 1-arc launcher and a final 3-arc launcher, with or without a 2-arc launcher, as in sentences like (53a), which correspond to independent clauses like (53b):

(53) a. Marcel leur fera écrire (des lettres) à Jules.
"Marcel will make them write (letters) to Jules."
b. Ils écriront (des lettres) à Jules.
"They will write (letters) to Jules."

The relevant PN would determine a box diagram like (54):

(54)

Marcel	leur	(des lettres)	(à) Jules
1	3	2	R_x
1	9	2	3
1	9	9	9
	1	2	3

Significantly, Postimage Principles A and B1 combine with the French rule (42a) to determine that BOTH the complement 1 and 3 head 3-arc postimages. The Stratal Uniqueness Law (see Perlmutter and Postal 1983) guarantees that these cannot both be members of any single stratum, in particular not the main clause final stratum. Therefore, one or the other of the 3-arc postimages must itself have a local successor.[12] In (54) it is claimed that it is the postimage of the 3-arc which has a successor, whose R-sign is not specified. Such structures and their many complex properties are discussed in detail in Postal (to appear b). The key point is that (54) shows how the recognition of 9-arc CU-images (for Term-arcs) permits JOINT maintenance of a maximally general law like Postimage Principle A and the Stratal Uniqueness Law. This is possible even in an NL like French, where initial 1-arc launchers are claimed to have 3-arc postimages, because the intermediate 9-arc CU-images permit avoidance of stratal uniqueness violations.

Although very many points relevant to the APG framework itself and to its application to the CIC have been left sketchy or passed over in silence, it should be relatively clear how the framework sketched in this section applies rather elegantly to the CIC, determining as lawful certain basic properties of this construction. Further specification of the relation between the theory and the CIC is provided in chapter 3.

Three

The Inversion Hypothesis

3.1 Formulating FC and the Passive Analysis of Certain CIC Complements

Given the CU account of the CIC sketched in chapter 2, one can consider more closely the nature of FC. Internal to the framework outlined in chapter 2, the French rule called FC can be stated in general (that is, lexically unrestricted) if somewhat informal terms as in (56):

(56) FC (Informal Statements)
  a. The head of the postimage of a 2-arc is plain. (First Version)
  b. The head of the postimage of an arc ACCUSATIVE at c_{final} is plain. (Final Version)

Rule (56) need not specify any R-sign for the postimage mentioned, since the theory of CU structures in chapter 2 entails that the postimage of a 2-arc is itself a 2-arc. Hence it is a theorem that any postimage instantiating the condition(s) in (56) is a 2-arc. For most data known to me, and all considered so far, the slightly simpler formulation (56a) suffices. But certain facts dealt with in sections 3.3, 3.4, and 4.4, involving the possibility of unaccusative CIC complement clauses WITHOUT final 1s, seem to require something like (56b), as discussed there.

As defined in Johnson and Postal (1980: 231), arc D in a stratum $c_k\langle b\rangle$ is ACCUSATIVE AT $c_k\langle b\rangle$ if and only if D is a 2-arc and there is a 1-arc in $c_k\langle b\rangle$. Recalling the discussion of launchers, (56a) imposes the constraint in the case of any 2-arc launcher at all, while (56b) imposes it in the narrower class of cases where a 2-arc cooccurs with a 1-arc launcher. The two intensionally distinct formulations can only differ extensionally if some 2-arc launchers are not neighbors of 1-arc launchers. For the moment, one can assume the two are equivalent and equate 'FC' with (56a).

Principle (56) claims that a CIC structure like (57), arc G must be plain.

(57)

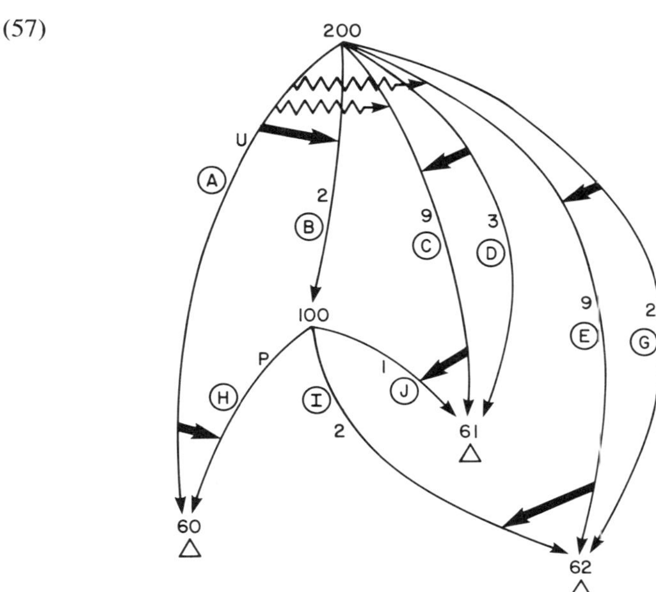

This means that G's head must be third person and that G must not be anaphorically connected to any neighboring arc, that is, to any other arc with tail node 200. It has of course not been formally specified what it means for the head of an arc to be third person. This notion can safely be left informal here, with the interpretation that an arc is third person unless its head corresponds to some non–third person pronoun or some conjunction one of whose conjuncts is a non–third person pronoun. But see chapter 5, where the problem of characterizing person emerges in an unsuspected way.

Distinct from (56), but nearly equivalent in its factual consequences, would be a statement like (58):

(58) The head of a 2-arc launcher is plain.

But (56) is chosen over (58) as the proper French rule because of the ungrammaticality of cases like *(59), which (58), unlike (56), would fail to block.

(59) *Hervé se fera critiquer/choisir/oublier à Louise.
"Herve$_i$ will make Louise criticize/choose/forget himself$_i$."

For in these the launcher is not fancy, since it is not reflexive, while the postimage in the main clause is fancy, since it is reflexive. This follows from the fact that the initial 1- and 2-arcs of the complement do not overlap in (59), while the initial 2-arc of the complement does overlap the main-clause initial 1-arc. So the 2-arc postimage in (59) is anaphorically connected to the main-clause 1-arc headed by *Hervé*.

At issue here is the APG assumption, discussed at length in Johnson and

Postal (1980: chapter 11) and in Aissen (1987), that 'coreference' is represented by overlapping self-sponsoring (initial) arcs, with anaphoric pronouns corresponding to the heads of noninitial arcs of a certain type. The latter, called REPLACERS, are cosponsored by some pair of overlapping initial arcs. Hence a typical 'coreference' structure would be (60b) for (60a), and in such terms the relevant structure of *(59) would be (60c).

(60) a. Jack criticizes himself.

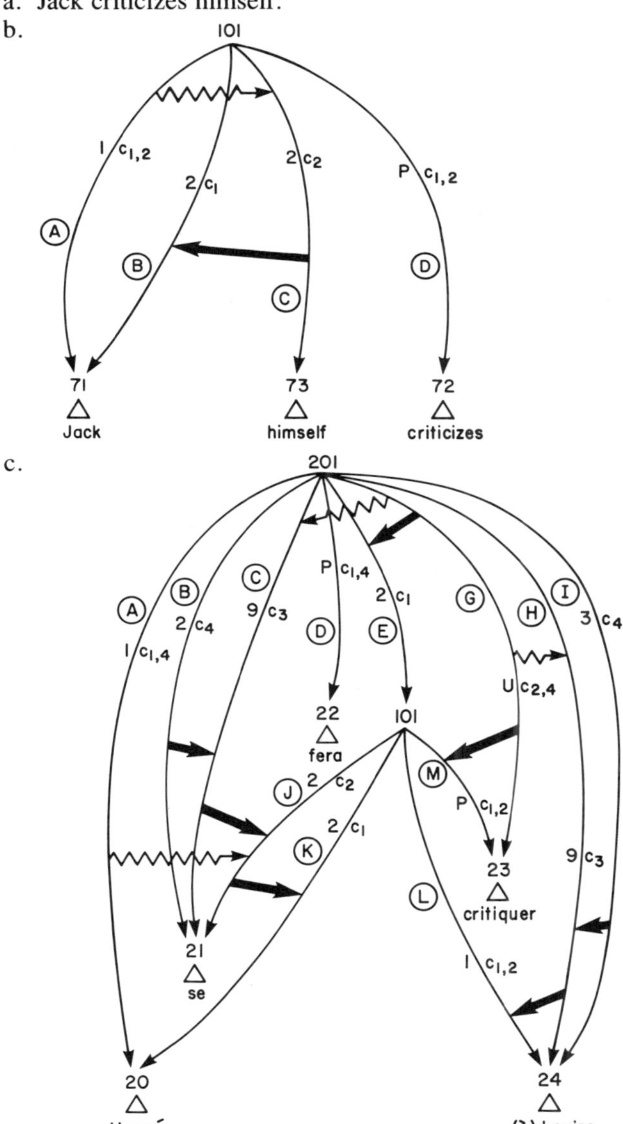

In (60b), A and B are initial overlapping arcs, and C is a replacer of B cosponsored by A and B and erasing B. Thus in (60c), arc J, a pronominal replacer, is nonetheless NOT reflexive, because its second sponsor, A, is not a neighbor of J. But B, J's pronominal postimage, is reflexive, because it is a neighbor of A. This provides an account of how the CU structure, with its determination of CU-images and postimages, determines the reflexive character of what would otherwise have been a nonreflexive pronoun (that corresponding to the head of arc B). Informally, these remarks amount essentially only to noting that the complement of a case like *(59) corresponds to an independent clause with no reflexive element, that is, schematically to (61):

(61) ⟨Louise$_i$ critiquer lui$_j$⟩

Principle (56) provides the basis of an effective answer to why FC systematically fails to exclude examples like (8) above and (62):

(62) a. Arnaud se/te/nous/vous fera critiquer/choisir/oublier par Louise.
"Arnaud will have himself/you/us/you criticized/chosen/forgotten by Louise."
b. On te/nous/vous a fait détester de tous.
"One had/got you/us/you detested by everyone."
c. On s'est fait détester de tous.
"One had/got oneself detested by everyone."

In these, the apparent superficial 1 of an apparently reflexive CIC complement appears not as a main-clause 3 but rather is marked in the same way as the former 1 of a personal passive clause with the same Vs; compare (9). The answer follows once one takes such sentences to involve, not embedded active clauses, but, as already indicated in section 2.2, embedded (personal) nonreflexive passives. Under this assumption, the relevant structure of the third variant of (62a) is (63). This structure ignores the fact that *nous* is a PC (just as (55c) ignored the fact that *se* is a PC), as well as the structure associated with the preposition *par.* In general, all succeeding PN representations will also ignore the status of PCs and treat them as if they were full nominals. This has no bearing on the argument. For some remarks on the actual description of PCs in APG terms, see Postal (1985, to appear a, to appear b).

(63)

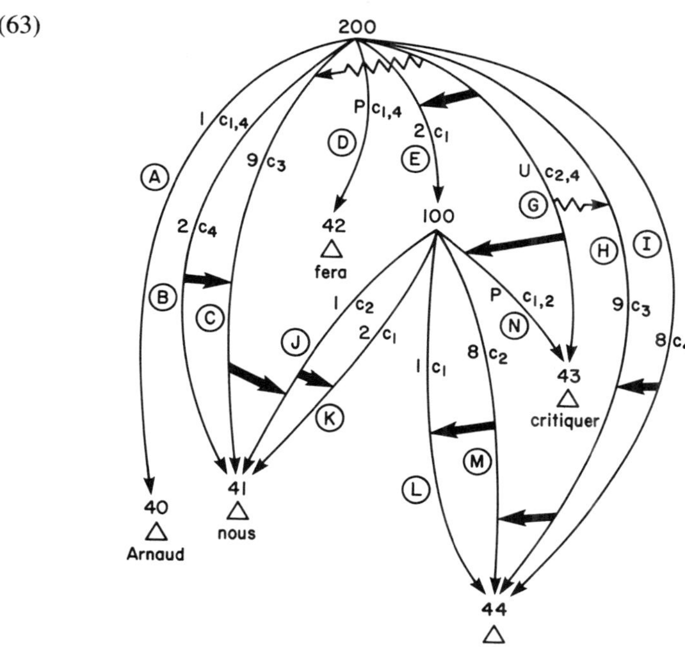

Significantly, (63) does not involve a fancy postimage of a 2-arc launcher, since it contains no 2-arc launcher at all. The only launchers are J and M. Under the personal passive analysis, the fancy element in the main clause corresponds to the final 1-arc of the complement, not to its final 2-arc, and FC is vacuously satisfied. In other words, the only 2-arc postimage in (63), B, is the postimage of a 1-arc (J). Note that this result is independent of the choice between (56a,b) as the proper formulation of FC.

A personal passive analysis of examples such as (62) like that in (63) provides an account of various correlations between such sentences and independent passives, many noted by Kayne (1975: chapter 3.5). One of the latter is the fact that the choice of preposition is identical in both:

(64) a. Arnaud a été critiqué par/*de Louise.
"Arnaud was criticized by Louise."
b. Arnaud s'est fait critiquer par/*de Louise.
"Arnaud had himself/got criticized by Louise."
c. On est détesté *par/de tous.
"One/we is/are detested by everyone."
d. On vous fera détester *par/de tous.
"One/we will have you be detested by everyone."

Despite such correlations, a personal passive analysis of the complements of cases like (62) is far from universally accepted.[1] One continuing basis for skepticism has been the absence from cases like (62) of the verbal morphology normally associated with (nonreflexive) passive clauses. That is, neither the passive auxiliary V *être* nor past participle morphology on the 'passive' V are present in (63), and both are entirely impossible:

(65) a. *Arnaud s'est fait (être) critiqué par Louise.
"Arnaud had himself/got criticized by Louise."
b. *On vous fera (être) détesté de tous.
"One/we will have you be detested by everyone."

But Postal (1985) develops an analysis in which a quite simple rule predicts the presence of this morphology in cases like (64a,c) and its absence in (64b,d), even given a passive analysis of the latter.[2] Thus I think this standard objection is not a real argument against a passive analysis.

However, more recent investigations, including Legendre (1986, to appear b), Perlmutter (1986a), and some of my own work, indicate rather clearly that as such, passive analyses along the lines of e.g. (48) for (47a) or (63) for the third variant of (62a) are not ENTIRELY correct. Although I will not go into detail, this work indicates that the underlying 2 of the complement in cases like (47a) and (62a) is not the FINAL 1 of that complement. Assuming this, the authors just mentioned have proposed relatively radical NONPASSIVE analyses of complements like that in (47a). For Legendre (1986), such complements consist of simple active clauses with no local successors. Perlmutter (1986a), after arguing against this proposal, suggests instead that the complement involves so-called 'spontaneous demotion', that is, an 8-arc local successor of the earlier 1-arc but no local successor for the earlier 2-arc. Perlmutter's proposal thus involves abandoning the RG/APG Motivated Chômage Law (see Perlmutter and Postal 1983) as well as a weakening of the Final 1-Arc Law.

However, a distinct innovative relational proposal incorporates the realization that the earlier complement 2 in (47a) is not a final 1, while maintaining both a passive structure and the Motivated Chômage Law. This proposal provides analysis (66) for (47a):

(66)	Louise	la voiture	(par) Jacques
	1	2	8
	1	9	9
	1	—	—
		2	8
		1	8
		2	1

Structure (66) differs from a standard RG/APG passive structure like (48) in only one way: the 1-arc local successor defining the complement as a passive clause itself has a 2-arc local successor. This determines that the clause has no final 1-arc. Such a state of affairs would be permitted if, as suggested in Fauconnier (1983) and Legendre (1986) and discussed further below, the Final 1-Arc Law is weakened so as not to require a final 1-arc in clause union complements. Thus the complement clause in (66) is a hitherto-unrecognized type of passive structure, one which can have no independent clause correspondent, since such a clause would violate even the weakened Final 1-Arc Law.

Structures like (66) interact with FC in essentially the same way as those like (48). The only difference is that whereas those like (48) are neutral with respect to the choice of formulations of FC as (56a) or (56b), (66), like other considerations brought up below, requires the choice of (56b). For clearly in the version of (63) in accord with the newer proposal, the passive 1-arc J in (63) would have a 2-arc local successor, and the latter, not the former, would be a launcher having a 2-arc postimage. If this 2-arc postimage is to satisfy FC, the latter can clearly not preclude all fancy 2-arc postimages of 2-arcs. But the version of (63) as altered to conform to the proposal which yields (66) instead of (48) would be consistent with FC taken as principle (56b). For under this proposal, the 2-arc local successor of the passive 1-arc would NOT be accusative at c_{final}.

I conclude that the complements of cases like (47a) and (62a) ARE passive clauses, but those of the hitherto-unrecognized type represented in (66). This is consistent with all of the arguments linking such complements to independent nonreflexive passive clauses, consistent with almost all the evidence accumulated by Legendre, Perlmutter, and others showing that the earlier 2 of cases like these is not a final 1, consistent with FC, consistent with the Motivated Chômage Law, and consistent with the strongest version of the Final 1-Arc Law that is independently viable (see section 4.4).[3]

Recognition that the complements of cases like (47a) have structures like (66) rather than like (48) raises an important question about rules, namely, that some rule which is consistent with structures like (66) must block French structures like (48).[4] Given that the relevant rule must not block those nonreflexive passives which are not CU complements, an obvious suggestion is that French has a rule which precludes a passive 1-arc from being a launcher, where by a 'passive' 1-arc I mean a 1-arc local successor which OVERRUNS an earlier 1-arc, thus one which is ARC-PASSIVE in the sense of Postal (1986a).[5] One arc A overruns another arc B if and only if they are neighbors, they have the same R-sign, and A's first coordinate index is +1 of B's last.

3.2 An Account of Nonstandard Complements Analogous to a Passive Analysis

Returning to nonstandard CIC sentences, the natural suggestion is that these should be analyzed in a way relevantly parallel to those like (62). The key feature of the passive analysis of the complements of the latter is that although these involve initially transitive clauses, there is no (c_{final} accusative) 2-arc launcher, and the underlying 1 does not head a 1-arc launcher. Rather, the launchers in cases like (62) are, given adoption of structures like (66), the 2-arc local successor of the passive 1-arc local successor of the earliest 2-arc and the 8-arc local successor of the earliest 1-arc. This follows from general principles touched on in section 2.2, according to which local predecessors and, more generally, arcs erased internal to the complement, can never be launchers. It should then be claimed that in nonstandard CIC sentences, the fancy main clause elements just do NOT head postimages of (accusative at c_{final}) 2-arcs. This approach might seem impossible, because the complements of nonstandard CIC cases are evidently NOT passives of any sort. But another clausal structure type long recognized in RG work permits development of an analysis of the desired type, namely, INVERSION structures, which are defined by the presence of 3-arc local successors of 1-arcs. There are several basic types of inversion clause—personal, impersonal, and, as suggested below, those in which there is no 1-arc in any postinversion stratum. I refer to the latter type as ABSOLUTE inversion structures.

In a standard personal inversion structure, a 1-arc of a transitive stratum has a 3-arc local successor, while a 2-arc of that stratum has a 1-arc local successor. This clause type is then defined by a representation including the features in (67).[6]

(67)

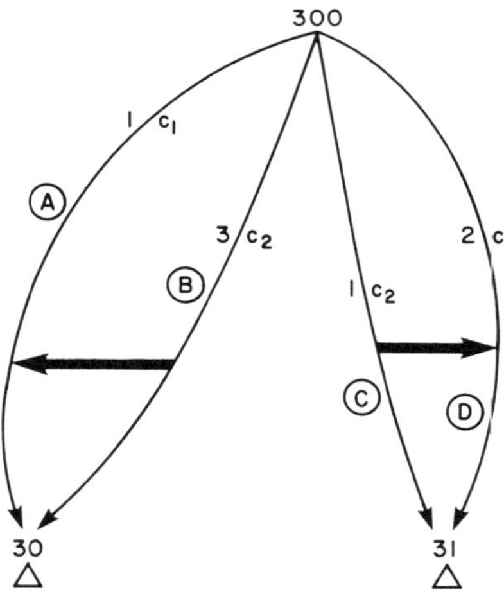

While I believe there are UNEMBEDDED French personal inversion clauses, their analysis as inversion structures is in general far from straightforward or obvious.[7] But personal inversion has been argued by Harris (1981) to be highly productive in Georgian, and arguments justifying personal inversion structures in Albanian, Choctaw, Italian, Japanese, Kannada, Spanish, and other NLs are found in the RG literature, which includes Davies (1981a, 1981b, 1984), Dryer (1982), Gonzalez (1985, 1986, to appear), Harris (1981, 1984a, 1984b), Hubbard (1980, 1981), Jackson (1982), Perlmutter (1984), Perlmutter and Postal (1984a), and many other references in Dubinsky and Rosen (1987).

To show how inversion is relevant to the analysis of nonstandard CIC sentences, one must consider in greater detail an important RG idea touched on earlier, namely, the UNACCUSATIVE HYPOTHESIS. This claims inter alia that INTRANSITIVE predicates divide into two types, UNERGATIVES and UNACCUSATIVES. The former occur with initial 1-arcs, and the latter with initial 2-arcs.[8] In a simple intransitive clause based on an unaccusative V, the final 1 will head a 1-arc local successor of a 2-arc. This is already illustrated by the complement in (51a) above. And I assume that a simple unaccusative structure also characterizes examples like (68):[9]

(68) a. Le medecin est sorti.
"The doctor went out."
b. La môme a disparu.
"The (female) kid disappeared."
c. Marie arrivera demain.
"Marie will arrive tomorrow."

A priori, nothing prevents either unergative or unaccusative intransitives from cooccurring with 3s. And both possibilities are, I claim, realized in French.

(69) a. Le spectre a répondu à Georges.
"The ghost replied to Georges."
b. Le spectre a apparu à Georges.
"The ghost appeared to Georges."
c. Le spectre lui a répondu/apparu.
"The ghost replied/appeared to hir."

Various considerations argue that (69a) involves an unergative structure but (69b) an unaccusative one. For instance, given the RG/APG 1 Advancement Exclusiveness Law (1AEX), this analysis properly predicts that (69b) has no corresponding IMPERSONAL passive, while it is consistent with the fact that (69a) does.[10] The 1AEX was introduced and discussed in Perlmutter and Postal (1984a) and is defended at length in Postal (1986a). It claims that no clause can contain more than a single 1-arc local successor.

(70) a. Il a été répondu à Georges par le spectre.
"It was replied to Georges by the ghost."
b. *Il a été apparu à Georges par le spectre.
"It was appeared to Georges by the ghost."

The 1AEX makes the right prediction about *(70b) on the assumption, defended in Perlmutter and Postal (1984a) and Postal (1986a), that impersonal passives are defined by the advancement to 1 of a dummy 2. If so, then the 1AEX predicts such passivization cannot cooccur with the advancement of an unaccusative 2 to 1, which, by the unaccusative view, defines a standard unaccusative clause like e.g. (69b). Similarly, under the account of the EXI construction (see (34) above) in Postal (1986a), the analysis predicts properly that EXI sentences can correspond to (69b) but not to (69a):

(71) a. *Il a répondu à Georges deux spectres horribles.
"Two horrible ghosts replied to Georges."
b. Il a apparu à Georges deux spectres horribles.
"Two horrible ghosts appeared to Georges."

Under the analysis of EXI in (34), unergative structures like (69a) are incompatible with EXI as in *(71a) simply because they contain no underlying 2-arc to sponsor the dummy 2-arc defining this construction. Other arguments relevant to the assignment of contrasting unergative and unaccusative statuses are also available; see Postal (1984, 1986a), Gibson and Raposo (1986), Legendre (to appear b).

Consider the behavior of an unaccusative clause C with a final 3 when C is embedded as a CIC complement. Given the theoretical account of CU structures in section 2.2, C's final 1-arc (since it is the local successor of a 2-arc) requires, according to Postimage Principle B2, a 2-arc postimage, while the final 3-arc must, according to Postimage Principle A, have a 3-arc postimage. The relevant pattern is illustrated by French cases (72d,e,f):

(72) a. Un spectre a apparu à Georges.
"A ghost appeared to Georges."
b. Un spectre lui a apparu.
"A ghost appeared to hir."
c. Il leur a apparu.
"It/he appeared to them."
d. Cela fera apparaître un spectre à Georges.
"That will make a ghost appear to Georges."
e. Cela leur fera apparaître un spectre.
"That will make a ghost appear to them."
f. Cela le leur fera apparaître.
"That will make it/him appear to them."

As predicted, when a clause like (72a), (72b) or (72c) is embedded in the CIC, its final 1 appears as main clause 2 and its final 3 as main clause 3.[11] Hence in the terms developed in chapter 2, (72d) would have a structure like (73).

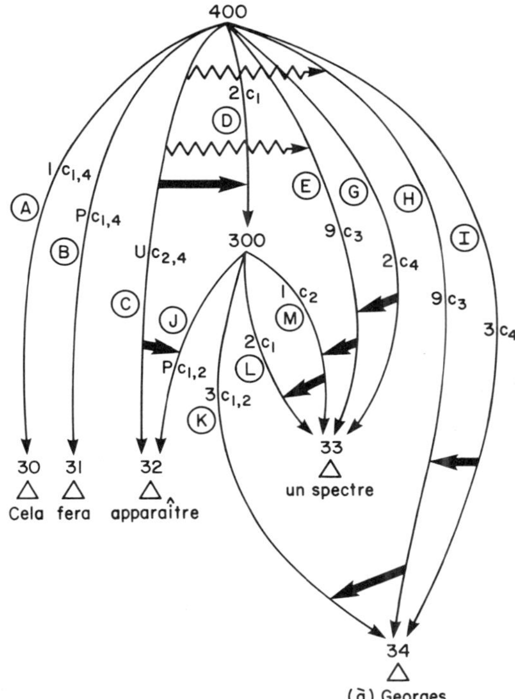

This determines a relevant box diagram like (74):

(74)

Cela	un spectre	(à) Georges
1	2	3
1	9	9
1	—	—
	1	3
	2	3

That the postimage G of the 1-arc launcher M headed by *un spectre* is a 2-arc is determined by Postimage Principle B2, while Postimage Principle A requires the 3-arc postimage for the 3-arc launcher K.

Note, incidentally, that standard RG/APG ideas require, via the Final 1-Arc Law, every basic clause to have a final 1-arc; see Perlmutter and Postal (1983), Johnson and Postal (1980: 227–30). In accord with this view, the complement in (73) is taken to involve advancement of the unaccusative 2 to 1. Nonetheless, the right pattern of postimages would be determined by the principles of chapter 2 even WITHOUT the advancement. For these laws determine that both a 2-arc launcher and a 1-arc launcher which is the local successor of a 2-arc have 2-arc postimages. So the present discussion is consistent with the possibility discussed earlier and later in several places that the Final 1-Arc Law does not hold for CU complements, hence not for the CIC under current assumptions. If this is correct, it could turn out that an example like (72d) is trivially structurally ambiguous, having both the structure in (73) and that in which the complement 2 does NOT advance to 1. Logically it would also be consistent with current assumptions if (72d) had a structure in which the earlier complement 2-arc has a 1-arc local successor, with the latter having a 2-arc local successor, which is the launcher with a 2-arc postimage.

Against this background, one can return to inversion structures. The key property of a personal inversion structure for current purposes is its lawful interaction with the CU principles sketched in section 2.2, in particular, Postimage Principles A and B2. Since, like an initially unaccusative one, such a structure contains a final 1-arc which is a local successor of a 2-arc, that 1-arc, if a launcher, must according to the latter law have a 2-arc postimage; the former principle specifies that if the inversion 3-arc is a launcher, it must have a 3-arc postimage. In short, given the theoretical account of CU structures in chapter 2, the personal inversion form of an earlier transitive structure will, when a CIC complement, behave just as an initially unaccusative intransitive clause containing a 3-like those in (72a,b,c). So a personal inversion complement should yield a CIC pattern parallel to (73).

Crucially then, the same principles at work in (72d,e,f) determine for a CIC complement which is the personal inversion form of an earlier transitive clause a pattern of postimages which is indistinguishable from the pattern of an embedded simple transitive clause. This observation was, in effect, apparently first made by Frantz (1977), who, however, developed it in a rather different framework and in the context of a hypothesis that NO CU complement could be a final-stratum transitive structure. The latter extremely strong hypothesis is, as made clear in what follows, disconfirmed by the facts of French. The postimage equivalences just noted are illustrated in the abstract NL-independent CU structure (75).

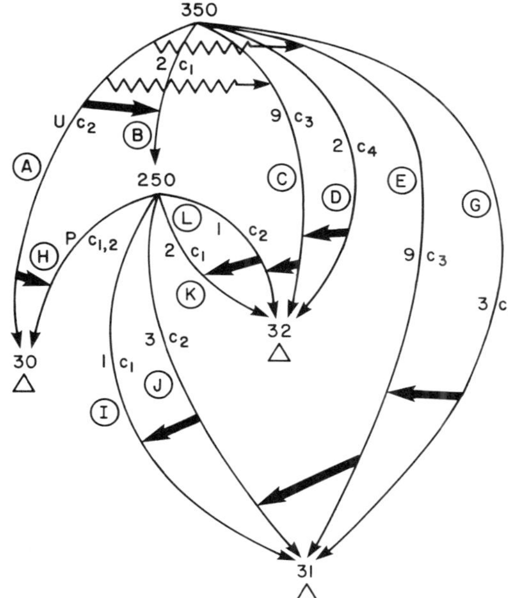

PN (75) shows that the postimage pattern for a personal inversion complement is the same in a specific sense as one for a complement in which the pattern of (local successor) relations defining inversion is not present. In each case, the framework in section 2.2 determines, with no special statements, that the initial 1 heads a 3-arc postimage, and that the initial 2 heads a 2-arc postimage. So in (75), node 31, the initial 1 of the complement, heads a 3-arc postimage, G, as a result of Postimage Principle A, while node 32, the initial 2, heads a 2-arc postimage, D, as a result of Postimage Principle B2. But if there were no inversion, and hence no arcs J and L, then I would be a 1-arc launcher and would have a 3-arc postimage via Postimage Principle B1 and French Postimage Rule 1, while the initial 2-arc K would be a launcher and would have a 2-arc postimage by Postimage Principle A.

More concretely, suppose, counterfactually, that the French transitive V *gifler* 'to slap' optionally occurred in independent personal inversion clauses. Alongside the actual (76a), one would then also find (76b):

(76) a. Jacques giflera Claudine.
b. HYPOTHETICAL
Claudine giflera à Jacques.
"Jacques will slap Claudine."

The key point is that the CU principles of chapter 2 determine that regardless of which of (76a,b) is embedded as a CU complement, the same nominals must head the same type of postimage; in each case, *Jacques* would head a 3-arc postimage and *Claudine* a 2-arc postimage. The only difference would concern 'intermediate' structures. In the standard transitive case corresponding to (76a), *Jacques* would head a 3-arc postimage of a 1-arc launcher, while in the inversion case this nominal would head a 3-arc postimage of a 3-arc launcher. Similarly, in the transitive case, *Claudine* would head a 2-arc postimage of a 2-arc, while in the inversion case, this nominal would head a 2-arc postimage of a 1-arc. In general such differences have no visible consequences. But they can have such in a particular NL if there are rules sensitive to one of the distinctions. Crucially, FC is just such a rule, since it distinguishes, in version (56a), fancy postimages of 2-arcs from fancy postimages of non–2-arcs and, in version (56b), fancy postimages of 2-arcs with neighboring 3-arc postimages of 1-arcs from those having neighboring 3-arc postimages of non–1- (that is, 3-) arcs.

Logically then, internal to the theory of CU constructions sketched in chapter 2, a CIC pattern like e.g. (44a), in which an apparently transitive complement yields postimage 2- and 3-arcs, has at least two possible analyses. One is the straightforward transitive analysis with both 1-arc and 2-arc launchers in the complement; another is the personal inversion analysis, in which the launchers are a 1-arc and a 3-arc. It follows that a CIC pattern like those found with French nonstandard CIC Vs MIGHT in part be a function of personal inversion in the complement. This assumption would yield the right pattern of main clause relations just as the straightforward transitive embedding assumption would. Given the anomalies shown in chapter 1 to be inevitably associated with the latter assumption in the case of NONSTANDARD Vs, it is then worthwhile to explore the following hypothesis: while standard sentences involve final-stratum transitive complements, nonstandard sentences contrast in having inversion complements rather than final-stratum transitive ones. This inversion would be 'masked' in the sense that the resulting identity of postimage patterns with that of standard transitive complements, which follows from the framework in section 2.2, makes complement inversion superficially invisible.

Observe that, exactly as in the case of earlier remarks about the advancement of the 2 to 1 in (73), the identity of postimage patterns just demonstrated is independent of the advancement of earlier 2 to 1 in an inversion structure, that is, it is independent of whether such a structure manifests personal or absolute inversion. Hence, if it is correct to weaken the Final 1-Arc Law so that it does not govern CU complements, as argued in Fauconnier (1983), Legendre (1986), and below, many CIC inversion structures could harmlessly turn out to be ambiguously either personal or absolute. Moreover, the identity of postimage patterns is independent of whether or not the 1-arc local successor in a personal inversion CU complement itself has a 2-arc local successor, for reasons identical to those brought out in the discussion of passive structures like (66).

Let us then hypothesize that the basic irregularity manifested by nonstandard Vs is not that they are exceptions to FC but rather that they are transitive Vs which are allowed to occur in inversion clauses, perhaps indifferently personal (with or without redemotion to 2) or absolute, for reasons just sketched, IF these clauses are CIC complements. Standard Vs like *critiquer, choisir,* and *oublier* do not have this option. Thus I adopt the view that the nonstandard Vs *(re)connaître* and *voir* can occur in inversion structures IF these are CIC complements, while standard transitive Vs like *choisir* or *critiquer* cannot occur in inversion clauses under any circumstances. More specifically, recalling that nonstandard sentences based on *(re)connaître* and *voir* are possible only with CIC main V *faire,* it is hypothesized that French has at least three Vs which can occur in personal inversion structures if those are the CIC complements of *faire,* although not in general otherwise.[12] Henceforth these assumptions are referred to as THE INVERSION HYPOTHESIS. This hypothesis remains vague about certain points, in particular, about whether the posited inversion is optional or obligatory in the relevant complements. This vagueness is eliminated in section 4.1.

Let us explore some immediate consequences of positing masked inversion for the domain of interest. First, the inversion hypothesis provides a direct account of the well-formedness of examples like (10a–d). If these have simple personal inversion clauses as complements, (10a–d) simply do not violate FC, interpreted as (56a), since their complements then contain no fancy post-images of 2-arc launchers. For as (75) shows, they contain no 2-arc launchers at all. Alternatively, even if the considerations about the possibility of CIC complements without final 1s are relevant, FC, then interpreted as (56b), is still not violated. There are then two possibilities. (1) The relevant inversion is absolute and thus the underlying complement 2-arc IS a launcher. But that launcher cannot be accusative in the final stratum. For the inversion 3-arc would erase its 1-arc predecessor, guaranteeing the absence of the latter from the final stratum; see note 13. So there is no way for an absolute inversion structure not to satisfy (56b). (2) The inversion might be personal, but with redemotion of the advancee 1 to 2. In that case also, there is no final stratum 1-arc and the demotion 2-arc, which is the launcher, is not accusative in the final stratum.

Next, with respect to facts like these illustrated in (25), repeated here, the apparent violations of RFX1 vanish under the inversion hypothesis.

(25) a. La psychiatrie a fait connaître Marcel à lui-même.
"Psychiatry made Marcel know himself."
b. Cela fera connaître ces gens l'un à l'autre.
"That will make these people know each other."

Since such examples can then involve inversion complements, the main clause elements *(à) lui-même* and *l'un (à) l'autre* are not final 1s but final 3s of the relevant complements. Hence RFX1 (= (30)) cannot be violated, that is, it is vacuously satisfied. But *(12a), also repeated here, is still bad, because under current hypotheses only nonstandard Vs can appear in the exceptional inversion pattern, and *critiquer, oublier,* etc., are STANDARD Vs.

(12) a. *La psychiatrie a fait critiquer/choisir/oublier Marcel à lui-même.
"Psychiatry made Marcel criticize/choose/forget himself."

So the complement of *(12a) must involve an RFX1 violation, since its *à* phrase has to correspond to the head of a final 1-arc launcher.

3.3 Absolute Inversion in CIC Complements

Initially less easy to account for under the inversion hypothesis are the marginal existence of sentences like (20b) and their contrast with those like (20a), both repeated here:

(20) a. *La psychiatrie a fait critiquer/choisir/oublier lui-même à Marcel/cet aveugle.
"Psychiatry made Marcel/that blind man criticize/choose/forget himself."
b. ?La psychiatrie a fait connaître lui-même à Marcel/cet aveugle.
"Psychiatry made Marcel/that blind man know himself."

One cannot suppose that (20b) involves a simple PERSONAL inversion complement. For in that case, the main clause *lui-même* would correspond to the head of a 1-arc launcher, hence to the head of a final 1-arc, and RFX1 (= (30)) would be violated in the complement. But neither can one suppose that the complement in (20b) corresponds to a simple final-stratum transitive clause, which would lead to conflicts with other regularities. Such an assumption would require a complement of the schematic form (77):

(77) ⟨Jacques$_i$ connaître lui-même$_i$⟩.

But as is well-known (see Kayne 1975: chapter 2) and is illustrated by *(78a), French clauses with a reflexive 2 anaphorically linked to the final 1 in general REQUIRE the presence of a reflexive PC; see (16).

(78) a. *Jacques$_i$ connaît lui-même$_i$.
b. Jacques se connaît (?lui-même).
"Jacques knows himself."

Yet the complement V in (20b) contains no reflexive PC. Further, the complement in (20b) can clearly not be taken to be a passive. One might imagine that the complement in (20b) could be some sort of IMPERSONAL inversion complement, that is, one with a dummy final 1. But section 4.3 advances grounds for the view that dummy 1s are impossible in French CU complements. Thus the proper APG structure of the complement clauses of marginal examples like (20b) is somewhat obscure.

But there are two subtly distinct hypotheses about this structure which are consistent with all maximal generalizations known to be possible for French independently of examples like (20b). The first is that the complement in (20b) is an ABSOLUTE inversion structure, hence one lacking any final 1. Under this view, the initial 1 demotes to 3, but neither the initial 2 nor any other element advances to 1. Such an analysis is only possible in a framework in which the Final 1-Arc Law of Johnson and Postal (1980) is weakened such that it does not require a 1-arc in the final stratum of a CU complement clause. This weakening assumption was already touched on in section 3.2 and is discussed in greater detail in sections 3.4 and 4.4 below. Significantly, such a weakening has already been suggested by Fauconnier (1983), who applies a nonadvancement view to various problems in French syntax, an idea further developed in Legendre (1986). Let us therefore adopt such a framework, that is, one in which the presence of a final-stratum 1-arc is not required in CU complements, hence not in CIC complements on present assumptions. See (215) below for formulation of a weaker version of the Final 1-Arc Law appropriate for this framework.

Then one current suggestion is that (20b) has, ignoring the tense auxiliary, a structure like (79).

(79)

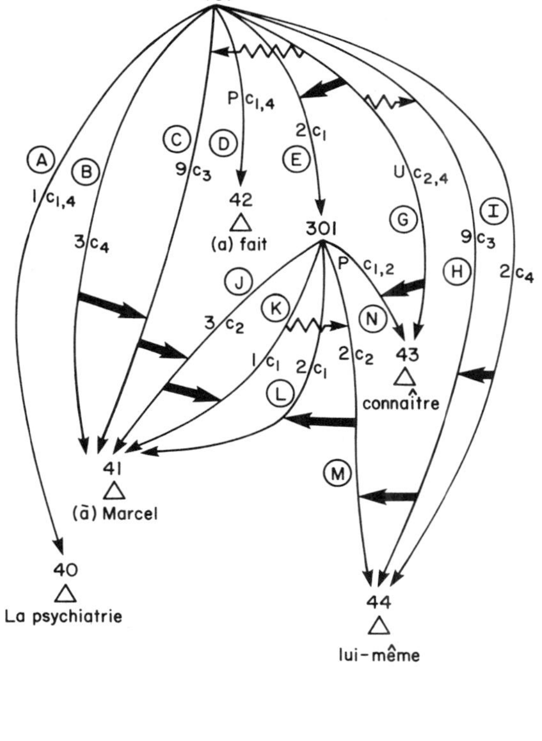

As an inversion structure, analysis (79) correctly predicts the status of the *à* phrase as a main clause 3, under Postimage Principle A. That is, this is just a standard case where a 3-arc launcher (here J) has a 3-arc postimage (here B). The same principle predicts that the final 2-arc of the complement headed by the reflexive pronoun, that is M, has a 2-arc postimage in the main clause, that is, I. Notably, (79) is consistent with FC, now interpreted, of course, as principle (56b), since the 2-arc postimage I is NOT a postimage of an arc accusative at c_{final}. This is true, since M is not accusative at c_{final} ($= c_2$). It is just the recognition of the inversion structure which makes this so, since it is the inversion 3-arc, J, which erases the initial 1-arc, K, and by general principle determines that the latter is not a final stratum arc.[13] Beyond passive complement structures like (66), it is those like (79) in particular which motivate the view that FC should be formulated as in (56b) rather than as in (56a), that is, by referencing finally accusative arcs rather than just 2-arc launchers.

The second and alternative hypothesis as to the structure of the complement of (20b) is that it is a personal inversion clause with redemotion of the advancee 1 to 2. This would yield a structure similar to (79), except that arc M would have a 1-arc local successor, call it X, and X would have a 2-arc local successor, call it Y. It is Y rather than M which would be the non-c_{final} accusative 2-arc launcher having a 2-arc postimage. I know of no evidence which currently could distinguish the distinct proposals involving absolute inversion from personal inversion with redemotion to 2. For present purposes, these proposals are effectively identical. This being so, they are henceforth not distinguished, and the term 'Absolute Inversion' is taken indifferently to subsume both inversion clauses in which there is no advancement of 2 to 1 and those in which there is but with redemotion to 2. Therefore 'Personal Inversion' henceforth excludes the latter case.

The beginning of this section observed in effect that although no principle explicitly precludes CIC complement PERSONAL inversion, this is nonetheless impossible in cases like (20b), because the result would violate RFX1. The null assumption is that there is no specific constraint on advancement to 1 in the presence of inversion. This would allow either personal or absolute inversion as in (79) in all cases which, unlike (20b), are NOT subject to some independent constraint, like FC, capable of either blocking the advancement to 1 or, conceivably, requiring it. Constraints like the latter are touched on in section 4.4. A consequence is that parallel to earlier remarks about the possibility of insignificant structural ambiguity in initial unaccusative structures like (72), present assumptions allow two partially distinct analyses for the CIC complement in a simple nonstandard example like (80):

(80) Marcel a fait connaître Lucille à Jacques.
"Marcel made Jacques know Lucille."

The first analysis involves absolute inversion, hence no advancement to 1, so that *Lucille* heads a 2-arc launcher which, by Postimage Principle A, has a 2-arc postimage in the main clause. On the other analysis there is personal inversion, that is, *Lucille* heads a 1-arc local successor, which is the launcher, and which, by Postimage Principle B, has a 2-arc postimage in the main clause. This structural ambiguity prediction is as far as I can see absolutely benign. Section 3.4 suggests, however, some reasons for thinking that the relevant freedom is found only with *connaître,* both *reconnaître* and *voir* being subject to a constraint which eliminates one of the possibilities.

An issue about examples like (20b) is the status of the reflexive *lui-même* in the MAIN clause. Structure (79) takes the main clause final (and surface) status of this phrase to be 2. There is something unusual in a French disjunctive REFLEXIVE form being a surface 2, in that in general a French reflexive 2 yields a reflexive PC and no disjunctive phrase. But it cannot be claimed that structure (79) requires recognition of an ad hoc anomaly in this area, a result that would count AGAINST the inversion hypothesis or against postulation of structures like (79).[14] For simple non-CIC cases like (19b) and (81) manifest the same property.

(81) ?On a décrit elle-même à Louise.
"One/we described Louise to herself."

So it can evidently be claimed that whatever principles allow (81) suffice to allow the non-PC reflexive in (20b). That is, it can be regarded as a brute fact about French, more precisely about that variety of French which does not reject cases like (81), that in some contexts reflexive 2s are allowed—in fact required—not to have PC realizations but rather to yield isolated full disjunctive reflexive nominals in *-même*. Therefore, for current purposes, which involve supporting the inversion hypothesis, there is no need to delve into the interesting issue of when a reflexive 2 must, can, or cannot yield a reflexive PC; see Postal (to appear b) for discussion of this topic.[15]

Cases like (81) are not relevant counterexamples to any otherwise viable laws governing anaphora, e.g. one which could preclude a surface 3 from anteceding a surface 2 in the same clause. For as shown in Hubbard (1980, 1981, 1982), 'coreference' between 2 and 3 in Albanian is apparently ONLY possible when the 3 is the antecedent.

The upshot of this discussion is that, granted that a relevant weakening of the Final 1-Arc Law is appropriate, the existence of the marginal possibility in (20b) is, under the inversion hypothesis, a direct consequence of whatever conditions allow examples like (81), in which a reflexive 2 is anteceded by a 3. The inversion account then predicts the impossibility of sentences like (20a), both for those variants which marginally allow (20b) and those which reject it totally. For the latter cases involve standard complement Vs, which preclude (any sort of) inversion. Therefore examples like (20a) must involve transitive complements and so violate the constraints which require that a reflexive 2 anteceded by a 1 determines a reflexive PC, not found in cases like (20a). That is, this account reduces the ungrammaticality of *(20a) to the independent principles which block non-CIC cases like *(82):

(82) *Cet aveugle$_i$ a critiqué/choisi/oublié lui-même$_i$.
"That blind man criticized/chose/forgot himself."

More completely, the present description reduces the contrast between *(20a) and (20b) to the contrast between *(82) and (81).

3.4 Differences between *connaître* and Other Nonstandard Verbs

Although *connaître, reconnaître,* and *voir* have all been categorized as nonstandard Vs, their behavior as CIC complement Vs is not uniform. This section explores the relevant differences with the goal of showing that they fail to undermine the basic conclusion of this study that nonstandard sentences all involve exceptional inversion complements.

Despite the well-formedness of (25a,b) and (20b) with *connaître,* repeated here, respectively, as (83a,b,c), parallel examples with *reconnaître* and *voir* are ill-formed, as shown in (84).

(83) a. La psychiatrie a fait connaître Marcel à lui-même.
"Psychiatry made Marcel know himself."
b. Cela fera connaître ces gens l'un à l'autre.
"That will make these people know (meet) each other."
c. ?La psychiatrie a fait connaître lui-même à cet aveugle.
"Psychiatry made that blind man know himself."

(84) a. *Cela fera reconnaître/voir Marcel à lui-même.
"That will make Marcel recognize/see himself."
b. *Cela fera reconnaître/voir ces gens l'un à l'autre.
"That will make these people recognize/see each other."
c. *Cela fera reconnaître/voir lui-même à cet aveugle.
"That will make that blind man recognize/see himself."

Nothing said so far accounts for this. One potential conclusion is to infer from the ill-formed cases in *(84) that *reconnaître* and *voir,* among nonstandard Vs, exclude the personal inversion structure I have postulated when either the inversion nominal itself or the earlier 2 is reflexive/reciprocal. For if *(84a,b,c) do not have inversion complements, that is, if they do have ordinary transitive complements, then their ill-formedness follows the same principles that block the parallel cases with STANDARD Vs: RFX1 (= (30)) in the case of *(84a,b) and the principle that requires the presence of a reflexive PC when a final 1 and final 2 are anaphorically linked in the case of *(84c).

If the rather straightforward approach just indicated is correct, then the rule(s) controlling the distribution of inversion with nonstandard Vs are less general than they otherwise could be. Aside from this though, the conclusion would not seriously impact the view that nonstandard complements involve inversion.

However, certain considerations might suggest, and to me do suggest, that the straightforward account of the contrasts between (83) and *(84) is not correct and that inversion in CIC complements is as free for *reconnaître* and *voir* as for *connaître*. The contrasts between (83) and *(84) would then have to follow from other principles. Focus first on the grammatical (83a). Notably, on an inversion analysis, (83a) is APPARENTLY anomalous internal to the account of reflexive 3s in Postal (to appear a). Although the arguments cannot be recapitulated here, considerable grounds are there advanced for the conclusion that in general French 'coreferential' reflexive 3s demote to 5 (Semiobject). If so, then *(à) lui-même* in (83a) would be a final 5 of the complement. Critically, it is shown that there is a constraint that the 3-arc local predecessor of a 5-arc cannot be a remote successor of, in particular, a 1-arc. This constraint would seem to be violated in (83a) under an inversion analysis, raising a serious problem for any attempt to integrate consistently the analysis of Postal (to appear a) and the inversion hypothesis of the present study. One conclusion, obviously, is that something is wrong with the account of the former work.

I suggest that there is indeed an error of sorts in that analysis, although one relatively peripheral to its overall set of assumptions. In that framework, it was assumed that while 'coreferential' REFLEXIVE 3s demote to 5, RECIPROCAL 3s in general demote to the distinct relation 4 (Demiobject). It now appears that Postal (to appear a) assumed too general an association between reflexive 3s and demotion to 5, specifically in the case of inversion 3s. This conclusion is supportable independently of any issues concerning nonstandard Vs on the basis of recent work by Legendre (to appear a, to appear b). Basically Legendre has shown that there is a class K of French inversion-determining Vs whose members are disjoint from those considered in my earlier work. The Vs in K include *convenir* 'to suit', *(dé)plaire* 'to (dis)please', *manquer* 'to miss', *nuire* 'to harm', *répugner* 'to disgust', and *ressembler* 'to resemble'. Legendre has developed a battery of arguments, chiefly but not entirely based on control phenomena of different sorts, which dovetail to support the inversion character of each member of K, in particular, the earlier 1-hood of their superficial 3s.

The key fact is then the following. The Vs in K are compatible with reflexive 3s, as illustrated in (85):

(85) a. Hervé s'est plait à lui-même.
"Herve pleased himself."
b. Hervé s'est nuit à lui-même.
"Herve harmed himself."

This being the case, it is not possible to maintain jointly all of the following assumptions of Postal (to appear a) and this study.

(86) a. 'Coreferential' reflexive 3s uniformly demote to 5.
  b. A 3 heading a 3-arc remote successor of a 1-arc cannot demote to 5.
  c. The 3s in (85) are inversion 3s, that is, heads of 3-arc local successors of 1-arcs.

I propose that the erroneous assumption is (86a), which is excessively general. I suggest that for reflexive inversion 3s, the standard situation is not, as I previously assumed, demotion to 5, but rather demotion to 4.

Actually, my earlier conclusion was really based on only three putative inversion-determining Vs, *falloir* 'to need, be necessary', *paraître* 'to appear', and *sembler* 'to seem'. These are indeed incompatible with reflexive 3s in a way which would be accounted for by the joint assumptions in (86):

(87) a. *Il faut Hervé à Lucille.
    "Lucille needs Herve."
  b. *Il faut Hervé à lui-même.
    "Herve needs himself."
  b. Lucille paraît/semble stupide à Jacques.
    "Lucille appears/seems stupid to Jacques."
  c. *Lucille (se) paraît/semble stupide à elle-même.
    "Lucille appears/seems stupid to herself."

However, in the light of Legendre's results, far from being the standard case for reflexive inversion 3s, the situation in (87) is unusual. A notable fact about these examples, in contrast to those involving the Vs Legendre has studied, is that in (87) the final 1s are NOT the result of advancement of nominals representing initial 2s.

Suppose that is nonaccidental, and that the actual demotion situation for reflexive inversion 3s is represented by the informal statement in (88):

(88) French Reflexive Inversion 3 Demotion Condition
  A reflexive inversion 3 demotes to 4 in clause C⟨b⟩ if and only if C⟨b⟩'s final 1 does NOT represent an initial 2 of C⟨b⟩.

Since all 'coreferential' reflexive/reciprocal 3s must, in the system of Postal (to appear a), demote to EITHER 4 or 5, (88) determines that in ordinary transitive inversion cases, like (85), reflexive 'coreferential' 3s will demote to 4. But the reflexive 3s in (87) demote to 5, determining ill-formedness via (86b), because the final 1-arcs in these sentences are not realizations of INITIAL 2-arcs. In the *falloir* cases, the final 1-arc is a dummy arc sponsored by the initial 1-arc (see Postal 1986a: chapter 3), while the final 1s in the *paraītre* and *sembler* clauses are nominals raised out of the complements, and thus not any kind of main clause initial constituents. A key point is that principle (88) is already required, independently of the analysis of nonstandard sentences, to save the account of Postal (to appear a) from the facts in (85), given the results in Legendre (to appear a, to appear b).

At this point, one can return to the problem of direct interest, namely, contrasts between (83) and *(84). Suppose one adopts the account of Postal (to appear a), as mildly modified just above, and also the view that inversion is equally free for all nonstandard Vs, rejecting what I earlier called the 'straightforward approach' to the (83)/*(84) contrasts. Then previous to the modification in (88), it might have seemed that *(84a) is entirely regular, being just another violation beyond those documented in Postal (to appear a) of the constraint precluding 3-to-5 demotion for a 3 which represents an earlier 1. However, given (88), this is no longer the case, since the final 1, if there is one (see below), in the complement of *(84a,b) would represent the initial 2. Hence such cases satisfy the conditions for demotion of the reflexive 3 to 4, not to 5, and nothing said so far blocks *(84a). This might not seem like progress.

But in any case, the ill-formedness of *(84b) would NOT previously have followed. The reason is, as already mentioned, that in the system of Postal (to appear a), reciprocal 3s, although also like reflexive forms subject to demotion, do not demote to 5 but a distinct relation, 4. Crucially, there is for 3-to-4 demotion no parallel to the ancestral constraint blocking 3-to-5 demotion with 3s bearing distinct earlier relations, in particular, no parallel to (86b). Hence 3-to-4 demotion with reciprocals is in general far freer than 3-to-5 demotion with reflexives. So there is no previous principle which would have blocked *(84b). But we have now set up a framework in which *(84a,b) involve the same phenomena, namely, 3-to-4 demotion. The question is why this is blocked in these cases, when there is no general ban on such demotion relevant to 3s which represent earlier 1s.

A potential answer is that the Vs *reconnaître* and *voir* are simply incompatible with 3-to-4 demotion. Although such a constraint is of course quite ad hoc, there are indications that French independently manifests such a condition. So the imposition of such a constraint on these two nonstandard Vs can apparently be a special case of one needed anyway. The basis of this conclusion is that the odd impersonal V *falloir,* argued in Postal (1986a: chapter 3) to occur in inversion clauses and already mentioned in connection with (87), reveals a pattern of ungrammaticalities which can be specified as incompatibility with 3-to-4 demotion.

(89) a. Il faut Jacques à ces handicapés.
"These handicapped persons need Jacques."
b. *Il faut ces handicapés l'un à l'autre.
"These handicapped persons need each other."

Example (90) illustrates the normal situation with noninversion Vs, (91) indicates that there is no general blockage on reciprocals in the case of inversion structures, and (92) shows that there is no general ban on a final 2 anteceding a reciprocal 3:

(90) a. Marcel et Marie-Claire se parlent l'un à l'autre.
"Marcel et Marie-Claire speak to each other."
b. Ces hommes se sont succédés l'un à l'autre (au poste de ministre).
"These men succeeded each other in the post of minister."

(91) a. Ces gens semblent stupides l'un à l'autre.
"These people seem stupid to each other."
b. Ces gens se plaisent l'un à l'autre.
"These people please each other."
c. Ces gens se sont manqués l'un à l'autre.
"These people missed each other."

(92) a. J'ai décrit ces gens l'un à l'autre.
"I described these (two) people to each other."
b. On a présenté ces femmes les unes aux autres.
"One/we introduced these women to each other."

Hence even on the assumption that *falloir* is an inversion V, the ill-formedness of *(89b) does not follow from any general principles, since reciprocal 3s normally demote to 4, a demotion not subject to conditions on the earlier relations of the demoted 3, as (91) illustrates.

Something special has to be said about *falloir,* and in the system of Postal (to appear a), the needed constraint can easily be regarded as a lexical incompatibility with 3-to-4 demotion. But then the constraints in *(84b) can be looked upon as instances of the same restriction. That is, *reconnaître* and *voir* would fall together with *falloir* in a class of Vs incompatible with 3-to-4 demotion, as in (93):

(93) French 3-to-4 Demotion Incompatibility Constraint
If A⟨b⟩ is a P-arc whose V-stem is headed by *falloir, reconnaître, voir,* or . . . , and B⟨b⟩ is a 3-arc, then B has no 4-arc local successor.

Thus the only specific additional cost to the grammar of blocking *(84b) would be listing the two relevant Vs in rule (93), whose overall structure is needed anyway. The examples in (83a,b) remain well-formed because *connaître* is NOT listed in (93), and thus the inversion clauses it determines are not incompatible with reciprocal or reflexive 3s, which can happily demote to 4, as required in effect by (88) combined with the claim that reflexive/reciprocal 3s in general demote to either 4 or 5.[16]

Turn now to the contrast between (83c) and *(84c). This cannot have anything to do with constraints on the demotion of reflexive or reciprocal 3s, since the complement 3s in such sentences are NONPRONOMINAL. Thus my discussion of the contrast between (83a,b) and *(84a,b) offers no help with this further difference among nonstandard Vs. A critical observation is that if the complements of *(84c) are just ordinary personal inversion clauses, then *(84c) is simply blocked by the general principle RFX1 (= (30)), since the complements would then contain final reflexive 1s anaphorically connected with final 3s. In these terms, the ungrammaticality of *(84c) is regular. The mystery is why (83c) is not blocked in the same way. The key to a solution is, I claim, the view developed somewhat in section 3.3, that the Final 1-Arc Law does NOT require a final 1-arc in CIC complements. It follows, as already indicated in earlier sections, that no principle of grammar REQUIRES that in a CIC inversion clause an earlier 2 advance to 1. This allows (83c) to have, rather than a personal inversion structure, as might have been assumed, the ABSOLUTE inversion structure already presented in (79). Notably, in that structure the reflexive form *lui-même* does not head a final 1-arc in the complement and hence cannot violate RFX1 (= (30)). While (79) indicates how CIC inversion complements based on *connaître* can escape from RFX1 via absolute inversion structures, a priori, the same sort of structure posited in (79) should then rescue parallel clauses based on *reconnaître*/*voir,* like *(84a,b). For nothing said so far distinguishes different nonstandard Vs in a relevant way.

One can, however, block *reconnaître*/*voir* in these contexts by assuming that these Vs are subject to a constraint which precludes them from taking advantage of the freedom allowed by the hypothesis that the Final 1-Arc Law does not require a final 1 in CU complements. The relevant constraint permits these Vs to occur only in clauses containing final 1s:

(94) Constraint on *voir, reconnaître*

If A⟨b⟩ is a P-arc whose V-stem is headed by *voir* or *reconnaître,* then ⟨b⟩'s final stratum contains a 1-arc.

It follows from this that clauses like *(84c) can only have structures in which the main clause 2 is a final 1 of the complement, violating RFX1. But (83c) can have a structure like (79) since there is no analogue of (94) for *connaître*.

While (94) is ad hoc, like my earlier postulation of incompatibility between *reconnaître*/*voir* and 3-to-4 demotion, distinct French data again suggest that the constraints are a special case of those existing independently. In this instance, the requirement of a final 1 is independently seen to be a constraint other French Vs are subject to. As first suggested in Fauconnier (1983), pursued in Legendre (1986), and discussed in greater detail in section 4.4, the contrast in the presence or absence of the 'inherent' reflexive PC in cases like (95a,b) can be attributed to the presence or absence of advancement of an unaccusative 2 to 1 in the CIC complement:

(95) a. Cela a fait s'asseoir la jeune fille.
     b. Cela a fait asseoir la jeune fille.
        "That made the young girl sit down."

However, the alternation in (95) is only possible with a proper subset of the unaccusative Vs which take 'inherent' reflexive PCs. Many such Vs only permit the variant in which the reflexive PC is PRESENT:

(96) a. Jacqueline s'est énervée.
b. *Jacqueline est/a énervé(e).
"Jacqueline got excited."
c. On a laissé s'énerver Jacqueline.
d. *On a laissé énerver Jacqueline.
"One/we let Jacqueline get excited."
e. Elle s'est mal comportée.
f. * Elle est/a mal comporté(e).
"She behaved badly."
g. On a laissé se comporter mal Jacqueline.
h. *On a laissé comporter mal Jacqueline.
"One/we let Jacqueline behave badly."

But to my knowledge no V taking inherent reflexives permits in CIC complements only the option in which the reflexive PC is ABSENT, as in effect noted by Johansson (1896: 105).[17]

These facts can be characterized if, following Fauconnier (1983), one claims that the option in (95) is simply due to the possibility of nonadvancement allowed by a weakened Final 1-Arc Law (see (215) below), and further, that blockages like *(96d) are due to the fact that some 'inherently' reflexive Vs, including *(se) comporter,* are subject to a constraint analogous to (94). More precisely, one should assume there is a single rule referencing all of the relatively few French Vs NOT requiring final 1s, yielding a replacement of (94) by (97):

(97) The French Final 1-Arc Constraint
If A⟨b⟩ is a NONPASSIVE P-arc and ⟨b⟩'s final stratum contains no 1-arc, then A's V-stem is headed by *asseoir, connaître,* . . . .

The dots in (97) schematically represent all other French Vs NOT requiring final 1s, a set containing *(se) taire* 'to be silent', but not *reconnaître, voir* or *(se) comporter.* The restriction 'NONPASSIVE' in (97) is required to keep this claim consistent with the postulation of passive structures like (66) above. These contain no final 1-arc, but are not sensitive to choice of V and are hence entirely independent of the restriction (97) is intended to impose.[18] I take these considerations to suggest the plausibility of rule (97), which, under the assumption that *voir* and *reconnaître* would not be listed in (97), entails the special constraint posited for these Vs in (94).

I will now conclude this discussion of the contrast between *connaître,* on the one hand, and *reconnaître/voir,* on the other, with respect to reflexives and reciprocals. The key feature of the current account is the following. I have argued that the contrast in question depends—internal to a system incorporating the general framework of Postal (to appear a), the inversion hypothesis, and the weakened Final 1-Arc Law—on essentially only two special stipulations. These are that *reconnaître* and *voir,* but not *connaître,* are listed as members of the V class in the independently motivated French constraint (93), and that only *connaître* among nonstandard Vs is listed in the independently motivated (97). The first specification precludes all inversion complements with the former two Vs in cases where the inversion 3 would be reciprocal or reflexive; the latter precludes inversion complements where the inversion 3 would antecede a reflexive 2, since it requires in effect this 2 to advance to 1, yielding a complement analysis which must conflict with RFX1 (= (30)). This provides initial justification for (97). One would, however, like to find other evidence suggesting that e.g. *reconnaître/voir,* unlike *connaître,* cannot occur in (CIC) clauses lacking final 1s. At present, however, I know of none.

The considerations of this section show, I believe, that it would be incorrect to interpret the contrast between (83) and *(84) as arguing against the overall inversion hypothesis advocated here. If examples like (83) did not involve inversion, that is, if they were ordinary transitive clauses, then several anomalies would have to be recognized, e.g. with respect to RFX1 and the principle requiring a reflexive PC in the case of anaphorically linked final 1 and 2. The analysis which seems to minimize irregularities is the inversion hypothesis, even given the need to specify an exceptional behavior for *reconnaître/voir* with respect to 3-to-4 demotion and for *connaître* with respect to final 1s. For given the facts about *falloir* in (89b), the former exceptionality reduces to nothing more than the listing of two nonstandard Vs in the independently needed (94), while given the facts about inherent reflexives, the latter reduces to nothing more than the listing of *connaître* in the independently required (97). Thus the contrasts between (83) and *(84) seem only to reflect the proper interaction of the inversion hypothesis with what are mostly independently existing constraints in French grammar. The key point is that the deleterious effects of a rejection of the inversion hypothesis would not be balanced by the provision of any help with respect to account for the contrast between (83) and *(84). More specifically, if (83a,b,c) are taken to represent CIC sentences with transitive complements, then there seems to be no way to reduce *(84) to anything other than entirely ad hoc constraints.

Four

Further Arguments for the Masked Inversion Hypothesis

In chapters 2 and 3, I developed a hypothesis as to the nature of apparently anomalous CIC sentences involving nonstandard complement Vs. This hypothesis is that these complements are inversion clauses, either personal or absolute, despite having main Vs which are ordinarily incompatible with inversion in non-CIC embeddings. No doubt some linguists would object a priori to the postulation, in restricted environments of a given NL, of abstract structures of a sort not generally productive in that NL. This sort of objection would reject the hypotheses of this study in principle. But the view in question seems to me to be merely a prejudice, with no known justification; see chapter 6, note 3. In fact, under most formulations, this type of objection threatens to be little more than question begging. Involved would be an argument of the form 'Feature F cannot be postulated in context X in language L because F does not occur in L'. Insertion of the word 'otherwise' before 'occur' here rescues the claim from question begging. But it yields an innocuous specification which fails to support the rejection of the hypothesis that F occurs in X. In all such cases, the nonoccurrence of F in other contexts can at best support a simplicity argument against postulating the presence of F in X.

It was shown that postulation of a masked inversion structure has several principal positive consequences in the case of nonstandard structures. The inversion hypothesis eliminates apparent anomalies with respect to several different principles of French grammar. These are FC (= (56)), RFX1 (= (30)), the constraint (not formulated here; see Postal to appear b) which requires that a final 2 which is LOCALLY anaphorically paired to a final 1 determines a reflexive accusative PC, and finally the principle that the final 1 of a CIC complement containing an accusative reflexive PC appears in the main clause as a final 2, not as a final 3; for the latter principle, see chapter 3, note 16 and chapter 1, note 2. Thus, (1) the inversion postulation permits maintenance of a simple and exception-free version of FC DESPITE the existence of grammatical sentences like (10a–d); (2) it allows maintenance of a maximally simple version of RFX1 like (30), despite the existence of (83a,b) and of their contrast with regular (nonstandard) cases like *(12a); (3) it provides, via recognition of absolute inversion, a means of allowing *connaître* sentences like (83c), while appealing to (93) to mark the ungrammaticality of *voir/reconnaître* structures like *(84a,b); (4) it offers a means of keeping examples like (83c) consistent with the grammar despite the ill-formedness of *(84c) and standard cases like *(20a), via appeal to absolute inversion and rule (97); (5) finally, the inversion hypothesis offers a means of maintaining (in spite of (ib) of chapter 3, note 16) the otherwise exceptionless principle that the final 1 of a CIC complement incorporating an accusative reflexive PC heads a 2-arc postimage.

Elimination of anomalies in independent constraints and subsumption of apparently peculiar sentences under independently motivated clause types are obviously good reasons for adopting the inversion hypothesis for nonstandard structures and, in the absence of known counterarguments, probably suffice to justify this step. But further sources of support for the inversion hypothesis inhere in the behavior of various 'adverbial' expressions.

4.1 Manner Adverbial Expressions

Consider manner adverbials (henceforth MAs) like *à regret, avec enthousiasme, avec plaisir,* etc. While overall constraints governing these are not entirely clear, certain contrasts suggest an incompatibility between them and an inversion nominal. This makes them potentially relevant to the goals of this study. But a disclaimer is in order. Although presumably the distributional conditions are relatively uniform for different MAs, I have systematically tested the environments in the text in general only with the three forms actually listed. For a list of many diverse MAs, see Authier (1972: 117–20).

Very informally, one can say that an MA must modify some nominal of the clause in which it appears and cannot modify others. So in (98) it is the referent of *Marcel* which is understood to manifest enthusiasm, experience regret, etc.

(98) Marcel a dansé pour Louise à regret/avec enthousiasme/avec plaisir.
"Marcel danced for Louise with regret/enthusiasm/pleasure."

The MAs cannot be understood as associated with *Louise*. In (99), the MA can be understood as associated with the nominal *Ma mère* but not with either *Louise* or *Jérôme:*

(99) Ma mère a décrit Louise à Jérôme avec enthousiasme.
"My mother described Louise to Jerome with enthusiasm."

Using the transformational terms common at the time, Ruwet (1972: 117) suggested that MAs must be associated with 'deep structure subjects'. This accounts for the associations and nonassociations in (98) and (99) and, importantly, also for facts like those in (100):

(100) a. Les policiers ont dispersé les étudiants avec enthousiasme.
"The policemen dispersed the students with enthusiasm."
b. Les étudiants ont été dispersés par les policiers avec enthousiasme.
"The students were dispersed by the policemen with enthusiasm."

In the nonreflexive personal passive (100b), as in the active (100a), the enthusiasm is manifested by the police, not by the students. This followed since, in the transformational terms of the period, the 1 of an active clause and the post-*par* phrase of a passive clause both corresponded to deep structure 1s.[1] 'Translating' into standard RG terms, Ruwet's observation would reduce to the informal principle that an MA in clause C must be associated with the INITIAL 1 of C. This works fine for (98) and (99) and for (100) where, in RG/APG terms, *les policiers* heads the initial 1-arc in both. The initial-1 assumption also works properly for REFLEXIVE passives like (101).

(101) Les vitres, ça se brise avec enthousiasme.
"Windows are broken by unspecified with enthusiasm." Ruwet (1972: 118)

For Ruwet, cases like (101) are grammatical because the MA was associated with the deep structure 1, under his transformational analysis of this construction. In current terms, (101) is well-formed for similar reasons, since this reflexive passive structure has an invisible initial 1.[2] Sentence (101) shows that the nominal associated with an MA need not have a realization in the surface form of a sentence.

Despite its evident virtues, an initial-1 analysis cannot be literally maintained if, as above, the unaccusative hypothesis is adopted for French. If French intransitives like *tomber, rester,* (*se*) *disperser,* etc., take initial 2s and not initial 1s, then the initial-1 hypothesis about MAs is false. For it is incompatible with the fact that MAs can be associated with the final 1s of these Vs, which are not, according to the unaccusative assumption, initial 1s. Compatibility between MAs and unaccusatives was already in effect shown by certain of Ruwet's (1972) examples and is systematically revealed by many others:

(102) a. Les étudiants se sont dispersés à regret/avec enthousiasme.
"The students dispersed with regret/enthusiasm."
b. Hervé est resté là-bas avec plaisir.
"Herve stayed over there with pleasure."
c. Mons fils est devenu un policier à regret.
"My son became a policemen with regret." (Ruwet 1972: 118)

Fortunately, facts like those illustrated in (98) cause no serious descriptive problem. For at worst a generalization governing both (100) and (102) is available via an easily defined notion of FIRST 1.

A first 1 is the head of the first 1-arc of a clause. The latter is a 1-arc whose first coordinate index is smaller than the first coordinate index of any neighboring 1-arc; see Perlmutter (1982), Marlett (1984) and Postal (1986a: 229). In any clause containing an initial 1-arc, that will be the first 1-arc. But a 1-arc local successor of an initial unaccusative 2-arc is also a first 1-arc. Hence this notion groups together the initial 1s of transitive, unergative, and passive clauses with the NONINITIAL 1s of unaccusative clauses like (102a,b,c), but properly separates all these from the final 1s of passives like (100b). Moreover, a first-1 analysis of MAs combines with the view of the EXI construction proposed in Postal (1986a: chapter 5) and in Postal (1986b) and illustrated already in (34) above to predict correctly an incompatibility between EXI and MAs in unaccusative intransitive clauses, one which may not have been previously noted.[3]

(103) a. Un homme est resté là-bas avec plaisir.
"A man stayed over there with pleasure."
b. Il est resté un homme là-bas (*avec plaisir).
"A man stayed over there (with pleasure)."
c. Deux gosses sont tout à coup sortis avec enthousiasme.
"Two kids suddenly went out with enthusiasm."
d. Il est tout à coup sorti deux gosses (*avec enthousiasme).
"Two kids suddenly went out (with enthusiasm)."

Under the first-1 analysis of MAs, the long forms of (103b,d) are ill-formed because the unaccusative EXI pivot, which heads an initial 2-arc, heads no 1-arc at all under the analysis in (34). The ungrammaticality of the long forms of (103b,d) supports the unaccusative treatment of the relevant Vs, as well as the treatment of EXI in Postal (1986a, 1986b). For taken jointly, these assumptions prevent EXI pivots from heading first 1-arcs.

A first 1-arc condition can also account for the fact that MAs are possible with both sorts of predicate nominal constructions in (104):

(104) a. Marcel est le directeur (à regret).
"Marcel is the director (with regret)."
b. Le directeur, c'est Marcel (à regret).
"The director is Marcel (with regret)."

Sentence (104a) is allowed under the straightforward assumption that the final 1 is the initial, hence first, 1. I believe the nominal in (104b) associated with the MA is *Marcel*. This is consistent with the fact that in (104b), as in (104a), it is *Marcel* who regrets. Consequently, one would have to analyze such cases so that *Marcel* heads the first 1-arc. This would mean an underlying analysis of the (104b) type similar to that of the (104a) type, which does not seem unreasonable. For APG analyses of predicate nominal constructions, see Johnson and Postal (1980: chapter 7), Postal (1986a: chapter 5). In these discussions, such constructions are taken to involve P-arc local successors of Nuclear Term

(1, 2) arcs. If so, then the first 1-arc condition for MAs could be met by taking (104b) to involve a P-arc local successor of the initial 1-arc, with *Marcel* then heading an initial (hence first) 1-arc and later P-arc.[4] The structure of (104b), if we ignore those features associated with the auxiliary *être,* would then be along the lines of (105).[5]

(105)

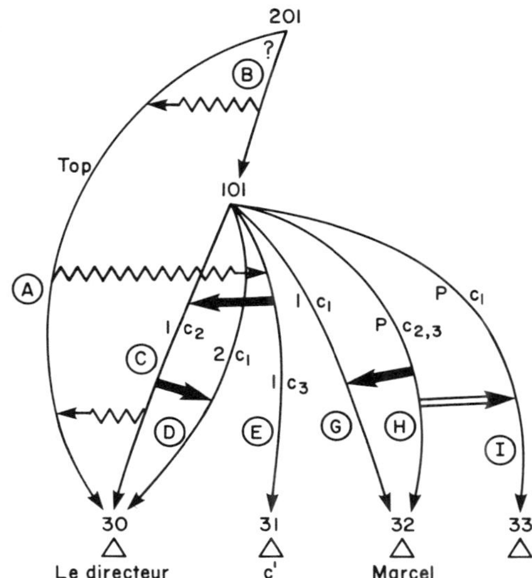

The assumption that a first 1-arc condition is a correct NECESSARY condition on the distribution of MAs is consistent with the association of MAs with inversion nominals, since these head first 1-arcs. But when there is some basis for analyzing a superficial 3 as an inversion 3, association with MAs nonetheless seems blocked, even in sentences which are largely synonymous with noninversion sentences containing the same MAs:

(106) a. ?Hervé a besoin de cela à regret.
"Herve needs that with regret."
b. *Il faut cela à Hervé à regret.
"Herve needs that with regret."

(107) a. Hervé a profité de vos ennuis à regret.
"Herve profited from your troubles with regret."
b. Vos ennuis ont profité à Hervé (*à regret).
"Herve profited from your troubles (with regret)."

(108) a. Le sadique a bénéficié de sa souffrance avec plaisir.
"The sadist benefited from her suffering with pleasure."
b. Sa souffrance a bénéficié au sadique (*avec plaisir).
"The sadist benefited from her suffering (with pleasure)."

(109) a. Il a eu cette idée à regret.
"He got that idea with regret."
b. Cette idée lui est venue (*à regret).
"He got that idea (with regret)."
c. Il croit à regret que tu le détestes.
"He believes with regret that you detest him."
d. Il lui semble (*à regret) que tu le détestes.
"It seems to hir (with regret) that you detest him."

Note that if (107b) and (108b) are inversion structures, as here assumed, then the RG/APG 1AEX Law mentioned in connection with (70) above predicts that there cannot be impersonal passives corresponding to such structures. This is correct:

(110) a. Il a été profité de vos ennuis.
"It was profited from your troubles."
b. *Il a été profité à Hervé.
"It was profited by Herve."
c. Il a été bénéficié de sa souffrance (par le sadique).
"It was benefited from her suffering (by the sadist)."
d. *Il a été bénéficié au sadique (par sa souffrance).
"It was benefited by the sadist (from her suffering)."

It is especially striking that *connaître* has a highly colloquial usage where it appears in what I take to be inversion clauses quite independently of the CIC. These sentences are subject to the requirement that their final 1 be *cela/ça,* normally anaphorically related to a topic or to a right-dislocated phrase. Such sentences have no impersonal passive correspondents.

(111) a. Le bois de Boulogne, ça me connaît.
"I am familiar with the Boulogne woods."
b. *Le bois de Boulogne me connaît.[6]
"I am familiar with the Boulogne woods."
c. *(Le bois de Boulogne,) Il m'est connu (par ça).
"I am familiar with the Boulogne woods."

Notably though, MAs are impossible in such putative inversion clauses:

(112) a. Je connaissais le bois de Boulogne (?avec plaisir).
"I used to know the Boulogne woods (with pleasure)."
b. Le bois de Boulogne, ça me connaissait (*avec plaisir).[7]
"I used to know the Boulogne woods (with pleasure)."

One conclusion, of course, is that MAs disconfirm the idea that any of (106b), (107b), (108b), (109b,d), or (112b) involve inversion.

Alternatively, one can conclude that there is a further constraint on the 1-arc associated with MAs. This must not only be a first 1-arc, but must meet a condition defined in terms of a notion related to ACTING 1-Arc; see Perlmutter (1982). Roughly, an acting 1-arc is a 1-arc which does NOT have a Term-arc local successor. My suggestion is that a French MA must, roughly, be associated with a first 1-arc which is a remote local predecessor of an acting 1-arc.[8]

This formulation is motivated beyond the considerations already referred to, because I assume that French has various types of ANTIPASSIVE clauses, including those in (113).[9]

(113) a. Hervé mange (avec plaisir).
"Herve eats (with pleasure)."
b. Hervé se critique (à regret).
"Herve criticizes himself (with regret)."

In an antipassive clause, there is a 1-arc with a 2-arc local successor which itself has a 1-arc local successor. In such cases, the initial and final 1-arcs can have the same head node and yet be distinct arcs, with only the former being the first 1-arc. If such an analysis is correct for (either of) (113a,b), then the final 1-arc of these—call it A—is the local successor of an intermediate 2-arc, which is itself the local successor of the first (because initial) 1-arc. A is then an acting 1-arc and a remote local successor of a first 1-arc. Hence association with an MA is properly NOT blocked.

(114) Informal MA Restriction (First Version)
An MA in clause C⟨b⟩ must be associated with the head of an initial arc A⟨b⟩ which is a remote local predecessor of both a first 1-arc and an acting 1-arc.

This formulation leaves it unspecified whether or not the first 1-arc remote local successor and the acting 1-arc remote local successor required to satisfy (114) are distinct arcs.

While possibly adequate, (114) is unwieldy, because it references three different arcs. A more elegant statement of the constraints is possible using the defined term in (115):

(115) A is (a) VEDETTE (arc) in a stratum c_k⟨b⟩ if and only if A outranks any other arc in c_k⟨b⟩.[10]

Thus a vedette of a particular clausal stratum is in general the highest-ranking nuclear term arc in that stratum and hence either a 1-arc or an unaccusative 2-arc. The definition of vedette in (115) is parallel to the definitions in Johnson and Postal (1980) of other relative terms such as (UN)ERGATIVE AT c_k, ABSOLUTE AT c_k, (UN)ACCUSATIVE AT c_k, etc. Essentially, vedette is the opposite of Absolutive. The latter picks out the lowest-ranking nuclear term arc in a stratum, while the former picks out the highest. One can then suggest (116) as an improvement over (114).

(116) Informal MA Restriction (Second Version)
An MA in a clause C⟨b⟩ must be associated with the head of an arc A⟨b⟩ which is vedette at $c_{initial}$ and the remote local predecessor of an acting 1-arc.

However, certain facts suggest that (116) is not quite correct. The restrictions in (116) allow for the fact, illustrated in (100b) above, that an MA can be associated with the earlier 1 of a nonreflexive passive clause appearing as an 8 in a *par* phrase. This possibility is also allowed for nonreflexive impersonal passives, as in (117):

(117) Il a été fait appel à eux par la directeur avec enthousiasme.
"An appeal was made to them by the director with enthusiasm."

However, as is well-known, with certain Vs the earlier 1 of a nonreflexive personal passive can, and sometimes must, appear in a phrase in *de*.

(118) a. Marie est aidée par/de son fils.
"Marie is helped by her son."
b. Ce livre est détesté *par/de tous.
"This book is detested by everyone."
c. L'étranger est surveillé par/de tous.
"The foreigner is under surveillance by everyone."

While the relevant judgments are quite delicate, it seems that for my principal consultant, association of the earlier 1 of a passive is NOT permitted when this nominal appears in a *de* phrase.

(119) a. Marie a été accompagnée par/de son fils.
"Marie was accompanied by her son."
b. Marie a été accompagnée par son fils avec plaisir/à regret.
"Marie was accompanied by her son with pleasure/regret."
c. *Marie a été accompagnée de son fils avec plaisir/à regret.
"Marie was accompanied by her son with pleasure/regret."

(120) a. L'étranger est surveillé par tous à regret.
"The foreigner is under surveillance by everyone with regret."
b. *L'étranger est surveillé de tous à regret.
"The foreigner is under surveillance by everyone with regret."

(121) a. Le roi a réussi à se faire obéir par/de tous.
"The king managed to get himself obeyed by everyone."
b. Le roi a réussi à se faire obéir par tous avec enthousiasme.
"The king managed to get himself obeyed by everyone with enthusiasm."
c. *Le roi a réussi à se faire obéir de tous avec enthousiasme.
"The king managed to get himself obeyed by everyone with enthusiasm."

While consistent with (116), the inability of an MA to associate with a passive 1 appearing in a *de* phrase does not follow from this rule. I suggest that we can make it follow from a slightly revised version by adopting the view of the passive *par/de* contrast suggested in Postal (1986a: 136). That view is that the contrast involves grammatical relations, and that while *par* phrases represent 8-arc local successors of the earlier 1-arc, *de* phrases reflect local successors representing a traditionally unrecognized relation called there Quasiobject (R-Sign = 6). Thus the contrast is attributed to the fact that under certain conditions the earlier 1-arc in a French passive can/must have a 6-arc rather than an 8-arc local successor.[11]

Assuming this, the way to make the constraint on MAs predict the incompatibility of MAs and passive *de* phrases is to refine the notion 'Acting X-Arc'. The original version of this idea picks out those X-arcs whose local successors, if any, are not Term (1,2,3) arcs. One can define related notions such that the relevant set of eliminated local successors includes 6-arcs (and possibly others recognized in the same way). Suppose then one defines informally the notion 'Strict Acting X-Arc' as an X-arc (presumably, but not necessarily, limiting the range of 'X' to Term-arcs) not having a local successor whose R-Sign is a member of the set including at least 1, 2, 3, 6 (but not 8). One can then predict the incompatibility of MAs and passive *de* phrases by revising (116) to (122):

(122) Informal MA Restriction (Final Version)
An MA in a clause C⟨b⟩ must be associated with the head of an arc A⟨b⟩ which is vedette at c_{initial} and the remote local predecessor of a strict acting 1-arc.

Significantly, (122) entails that an MA CANNOT be associated with an inversion nominal, since an inversion 3-arc is not a strict acting 1-arc (or even an acting 1-arc). Because the only 1-arc that an inversion 3-arc B is a local successor of has a Term-arc local successor, namely, B itself. Principle (122) therefore interacts with the inversion hypothesis central to this study to predict that those clauses suggested to involve masked CIC inversion should be incompatible with embedded MAs. This entailment will be relevant for supporting the inversion hypothesis to the extent that standard CIC structures are compatible with embedded MAs associated with the final 1 of the complement, which they are.

(123) a. Je lui ai fait manger cela avec enthousiasme.
"I had hir eat that with enthusiasm."
b. Sa rage lui a fait battre ses victimes avec acharnement.
"Hir's rage made hir beat hir's victims with fury."
c. Cela leur a fait accepter le compromis avec enthousiasme.
"That made them accept the compromise with enthusiasm."

In (123a), the MA can be associated ambiguously with either the main clause 1 or the final 1 of the complement; in (123b,c), because of the inanimacy of the main-clause 1 in each case, the MA can only be associated with the final 1 of the complement. These facts are consistent with (122) under the ordinary assumption that all of (123a,b,c) have standard transitive complements. For in that case, the nominal underlying either the PC *lui* or *leur* in these examples heads both a first and a final 1-arc in the complement, hence heads a vedette-arc with a strict acting 1-arc local successor.

Recall then, that the inversion hypothesis separates cases (124a,b,c) into two sets, with (124a) not involving complement inversion but (124b,c) representing absolute inversion complements.

(124) a. Cela a fait se connaître André.
"That made Andre know himself."
b. Cela a fait connaître André à lui-même.
"That made Andre know himself."
c. ?Cela a fait connaître lui-même à André.
"That made Andre know himself."

Noninversion reflexive or reciprocal structures with nonstandard Vs are, as expected on semantic grounds, compatible with MAs, as shown by (125):

(125) a. André se connait à regret.
"Andre knows himself with regret."
b. Ces mecs se connaissent (l'un l'autre) avec plaisir.
"These guys know each other with pleasure."

Notably then, the inversion hypothesis and (122) combine to correctly predict the following MA contrasts among essential paraphrases:

(126) a. Cela a fait se connaître André (à regret).
b. Cela a fait connaître André à lui-même (*à regret).
c. ?Cela a fait connaître lui-même à André (*à regret).
"That made Andre know himself (with regret)."

In current terms, (126a) is not blocked by (122), because it does not involve complement inversion. Rather, the complement is an antipassive structure whose final 1-arc launcher thus satisfies (122) in the same way as that in (125a) does. But (126b,c) both involve inversion and are thus both incompatible with (122). So an inversion analysis of nonstandard sentences blocks *(126b,c) via the same principle that excludes the starred longer form of the unimbedded (122b). Under an analysis of nonstandard sentences as containing ordinary transitive clauses, the contrasts in (126) are, however, a further unaccounted-for anomaly.

The same principles function to predict parallel contrasts in reciprocal nonstandard sentences.

(127) a. Cela a fait se connaître ces gens l'un l'autre (avec plaisir).
b. Cela a fait connaître ces gens l'un à l'autre (*avec plaisir).
"That made these people know (meet) each other (with pleasure)."

The pattern of facts is predicted, since, in current terms, (127a) involves an embedded antipassive clause which satisfies (122), while (127b) has an embedded inversion clause, which cannot satisfy it, because the first 1 of the complement is a final 3, hence not a strict acting 1.

The interaction of principle (122) and the inversion hypothesis with respect to predicting MA contrasts in NON-reflexive/reciprocal cases is rather complicated. This is shown by sentences like (128d,e), which reveal contrasts with those in (123) above:

(128) a. Le medecin les verra avec plaisir.
"The doctor will see them with pleasure."

b. Son ami nous a vu avec enthousiasme.
"His friend saw us with enthusiasm."
c. On les fera voir au medecin (avec plaisir).
"One/we will have the doctor see them (with pleasure).
d. Jacqueline nous a fait voir à son ami (avec enthousiasme).
"Jacqueline had her friend see us (with enthusiasm)."
e. Cela nous a fait voir au medecin (*avec enthousiasme).
"That made the doctor see us (with enthusiasm)."

Consider first (128d). This contrasts sharply with (123), in that the MA is exclusively associable with the main clause 1, not with *(à) son ami,* in spite of the fact, illustrated in (128b), that this nominal can, as a real final 1 of the complement V, associate with the relevant MA. Expectably then, the long version of (128e) is ill-formed, for there is no nominal for the MA to associate with. The restrictions in (128d,e) follow under an inversion analysis of these clauses, since these nominals then head inversion 3-arcs in the final stratum of the complements, precluding satisfaction of (122).

However, this argument potentially contains a serious gap, related to a question which has so far been ignored. To what extent is the CIC complement inversion posited by the inversion hypothesis optional or obligatory? That is, does this hypothesis claim that inversion in a CIC complement based on a nonstandard V is necessary or just a possibility? If the latter, then CIC sentences based on nonstandard complements have in general dual analyses, one with inversion and one with an ordinary transitive analysis like that of standard Vs.

As it turns out, the optional/obligatory question cannot be decided on the basis of data like that in (128d,e), for the following reason. Suppose inversion in nonstandard complements is just an option. Then, a priori, (128d,e) would each have two analyses. But independently of constraints on MAs, the ordinary transitive analysis is blocked, since on that analysis these structures have fancy (because non–third person) postimages of accusative (at c_{final}) arcs and thus violate FC (= (56)). The generalization is that even if CIC complement inversion is in general optional, it may in effect be determined to be obligatory in particular contexts because of independently existing constraints, which can in principle block one or the other analysis.

Consider then (128c). I have marked this as grammatical. Since it involves a nonstandard complement, the grammaticality must, given rule (122) constraining MAs, be due to a noninversion analysis. This supports the view that in general nonstandard inversion is just an option. Such a conclusion is perhaps further supported by the following observation. While I consider cases like (128c) to be well-formed, for the relevant reading where the MA is associated with the complement 1, over time my consultant has given inconsistent judgments. On some occasions it is accepted and on others rejected. This contrasts very sharply with examples like (128d,e). Cases like the latter are NEVER accepted when the MA is present, while those like the former are always interpreted with the MA associated with the main clause 1, that is, they are always analyzed as inversion structures. It is possible, then, that the variable judgments for cases like (128c) are due precisely to the ambiguity allowed by the view that inversion is in general optional. It may be that when a case like (128c) is rejected, it is being analyzed as containing an inversion complement, while when it is accepted it is being analyzed as having an ordinary transitive one.

This account leaves at least one question unanswered. It assumes that speakers will sometimes judge a structure as ill-formed when it has an ungrammatical analysis due to inconsistency with some rule R, even though it has another (well-formed) grammatical analysis consistent with R. Surely though, this is not uniformly the case for all R, as revealed by forms like the version of (128e) lacking an MA. If inversion is optional, this type of sentence would also have two analyses, one well-formed with an inversion complement and one ill-formed with a finally transitive complement, yielding a violation of FC. And yet such sentences are on no occasion judged as ill-formed. Thus the phenomenon of shifting judgments associated with (128c) and related to rule (122) contrasts with the consistency of judgments with respect to the short form of (128e), which are related to FC (= rule (56)). Perhaps this extragrammatical difference can be characterized in some way, e.g. as having to do with the linguistic nature of different rules or the centrality or perspicacity of their psychological representations. But such psychological questions are beyond the purview of this study.

The patterns in (128) hold for parallel cases with *connaître:*

(129) a. ?Ton père les connaîtra avec plaisir.
"Your father will know them with pleasure."
b. ?Jules m'a connu avec plaisir.
"Jules knew me with pleasure."
c. L'avenir les fera connaître à ton père (avec plaisir).
"The future will make your father know (meet) them (with pleasure)."
d. On m'a fait connaître à Jules (avec plaisir).
"One made Jules know (meet) me (with pleasure)."
e. Cela m'a fait connaître à Jules (*avec plaisir).
"That made Jules know (meet) me (with pleasure)."

Here (129a,b) are doubtful because of the existence of the colloquial expression *faire la connaissance de* 'make the acquaintance of', which would normally be used. Parallel to the situation with *voir,* (129d) is interpretable only with the MA associated with main clause 1, and the long version of (129e) is ungrammatical. Moreover, the judgments of (129c) also vary over occasions. In this respect, both (128c) and (129c) of course contrast sharply with parallel CIC sentences based on standard Vs. Examples (128c,d) and (129c,d) should be compared with contrasting cases such as (130), based on standard complement Vs:

(130) a. Cela les a fait choisir/oublier à Jules (avec plaisir).
"That made Jules choose/forget them (with pleasure)."
b. Cela leur a fait choisir/oublier Marie (avec plaisir).
"That made them choose/forget Marie (with pleasure)."
c. Cela la leur a fait choisir/oublier (avec plaisir).
"That made them choose/forget her (with pleasure)."

In these, the MA can always be associated with the main clause 3, and such examples are never judged ungrammatical. This is consistent with (122), since the final 1s of the complement with these standard Vs are vedettes, no inversion ever being possible with nonstandard Vs, even internal to the inversion hypothesis. I conclude therefore that NONSTANDARD CIC INVERSION IS JUST AN OPTION, although an option forced or precluded in certain cases by independent constraints.

Actually, the view that nonstandard inversion is just an option is supported by further rather obvious facts. If inversion were truly obligatory in all nonstandard CIC complements, then it would be predicted that nonstandard Vs could not occur in well-formed complements like (126a) and (127a), which I have interpreted as antipassive structures, and could not occur in complements like those in (131), which I interpret as passives and whose existence was observed by Sandfeld.[12]

(131) a. On a fait connaître cela par mon père.
"One had that known by my father."
b. Les Halles centrales—feraient connaître la maison des quatre coins de Paris.
"The central halls would make the company known to the four corners of Paris." (Sandfield 1965: 182)
c. J'en ai assez—de me voir protéger par vos petites camarades.
"I've had enough of seeing myself protected by your little comrades." (Sandfeld 1965: 184)

Although the analysis of the complements in (126a), (127a), and (131) is no doubt controversial, it is clear that none of these complements can be taken to be inversion structures. Hence the view that nonstandard inversion is obligatory is, if interpreted literally, untenable. It could at best only be taken, rather obliquely, as meaning that standard final-stratum transitive complements are not possible with these Vs. But there seems to be no motivation for this view as opposed to that which takes inversion simply to be an option allowed for these Vs in CIC complement clauses. Moreover, the obligatoriness view is incompatible with facts like the long form of (128c) and with similar examples dealt with below, which arguably involve final-stratum transitive complements based on nonstandard Vs.

Some facts concerning the compatibility of the nonstandard V *connaître* with complement clauses might seem to be inconsistent with the inversion analysis. As noted in Gross (1975: 149–50), in simple active clauses *connaître* is incompatible with (tensed) complements.

(132) a. Il connaît ce tableau/*qu'elle viendra.
"He knows that picture/that she will come."
b. *Tous connaissent qu'Hervé est venu.
"Everyone knows that Herve came."

But it would seem that this constraint, whatever it is, does not hold in sentences related to (132a,b), since, as Gross (1975: 150) observed, (133), which he took to be a passive, is entirely grammatical:

(133) Qu'Hervé est venu est connu de tous.
"That Herve came is known to all."

Accepting Gross's assumptions, suppose that the constraint in (132a,b) is, in informal relational terms, something like (134):

(134) If A is a final 2-arc of a clause whose main V is *connaître*, then A is not headed by a (tensed) complement.

Rule (134) blocks both *(132a,b) and yet is compatible with (133), since in (133), under a passive analysis, while the complement heads an earlier 2-arc, it does not head a final 2-arc but rather a final 1-arc.

Consider the question of embedding *connaître* clauses with (tensed) complement 2s as CIC complements, given the optionality of the inversion hypothesis. According to this, the CIC complements of such cases could have, a priori, at least three distinct analyses:

(135) a. A standard transitive analysis
b. An absolute inversion analysis
c. A personal inversion analysis

Evidently analysis (135a) is blocked by constraint (134), and analysis (135b) is too. For in an absolute inversion structure, the earlier 2 does not advance to 1 and ends up as a final 2. But (134) does NOT block a personal inversion analysis, since it does not preclude the case where an underlying tensed complement based on *connaître* appears as the final 1 of an INVERSION clause, for the same reasons that rule (134) does not block (133).

Thus the inversion hypothesis about *connaître* seems to predict that the constraint visible in (132) should NOT be manifest in the CIC. That is, it apparently entails that, barring some additional constraints, (136) is grammatical.

(136) *Cela a fait connaître à tous qu'Hervé est venu.
"That made everyone know that Herve came."

But the complement in *(136) is actually no less ill-formed than those in (132a,b). This is apparently unexpected under the inversion hypothesis, since

*(136) would appear to have a well-formed personal inversion analysis under which the underlying complement 2 advances to 1 in the complement, thereby escaping from (134) for the same reason as (133) does. Thus, so far plausible and/or justified assumptions seem to yield factually untenable results in the case of *(136), casting doubt on the inversion hypothesis.

However, this problem can apparently be traced down to an incorrect assumption, namely, condition (134). The only fact justifying (134) as against a simpler and hence preferable condition like (137), from which the specification 'final' has been eliminated, is the assumption that (133) is a passive clause.

(137) If A is a 2-arc of a clause based on the V *connaître,* then A is not headed by a (tensed) complement.

But if (137) rather than (134) is correct, then *(136) is predicted merely from the assumption that the tensed complement in *(136) is an initial 2 of the CIC complement.

It is thus important to focus on the claim, taken from Gross (1975), that (133) is a passive (corresponding to (132b)). This is surely incorrect in one clear respect, since there is good evidence that the form *connu* in (133) is an ADJECTIVE, not a simple passive participle. The evidence is that this form occurs in contexts like *semble* . . . , which permit adjectives but not passive participles.

(138) a. Cela semble evident/triste/ridicule/impossible/connu de tous.
"That seems evident/sad/ridiculous/impossible/known to all."
b. *Cela semble cru (par tous)/détesté (de tous)/prouvé (par Gödel).
"That seems believed (by everyone)/detested (by everyone)/proved (by Gödel)."

There is thus ground for the view that clauses like (133) have a status similar to that of English sentences like (139).

(139) That is/appears known to everyone.

If (133) is an adjectival clause and not a simple passive clause, then there is no reason not to adopt the simpler (137), interpreting its reference to 'V' to exclude adjectives, leaving open the possibility that the final clausal 1 in (133) is an initial 2. It follows, then, that the ill-formedness of *(136) has no bearing on the inversion hypothesis, since constraint (137) blocks such sentences and is consistent with the inversion hypothesis.

One should also inquire whether certain observations of Kayne (1975: 237) have any relevance to the inversion hypothesis. Kayne noted that there were anaphoric connection contrasts like (140), and that these correlated with the CIC contrasts in (141):

(140) a. Jean_i apprenda son_i rôle.
"Jean will learn his own role."
b. *Son_i rôle sera appris par Jean_i.
"His own role will be learned by Jean."

(141) a. Tu feras apprendre son_i rôle à $Jean_i$.
"You will make Jean learn his own role."
b. *Tu feras apprendre son_i rôle par $Jean_i$.
"You will make his own role be learned by Jean."

Kayne took these data as an argument for the passive character of the complement of cases like *(141b). One might assume that the constraint manifested in *(140b) and *(141b) precludes a possessive pronoun in a 1 from being anteceded by another constituent of the clause containing that 1, e.g., that the rule is informally something like (142):

(142) If A is the antecedent of a possessive pronoun P which is a constituent of the final 1 of clause C, then A cannot be a constituent of C.

The relation between (142) and the inversion hypothesis is then this. Suppose, contrary to what was concluded above, that nonstandard CIC inversion were obligatory. Then if (142) is the correct principle underlying *(140b) and *(141b), the constraint underlying *(141b) should ALSO be manifest in nonstandard sentences in any case where the only possibility is a PERSONAL inversion structure. For in that case, the possessive structure would have had to advance to 1 in the complement.

Moreover, it was seen, when I motivated rule (94) above, that *voir* can only occur in clauses with final 1s, hence only in personal but not absolute inversion structures. Therefore, if nonstandard inversion is obligatory, the constraint in (142) should be manifest in nonstandard sentences with *voir*. In fact though, it is NOT found with *voir* any more than with *connaître:*

(143) a. Marie a fait voir ses_i fautes à $Jacques_i$.
"Marie made Jacques see his own faults."
b. On a fait connaître son_i rôle à $l'enfant_i$.
"One/we made the child know his own role."

While one can account for the well-formedness of (143b) via appeal to an absolute inversion structure, the analogous move for (143a) is precluded by rule (94), justified earlier, which requires a final 1 in all *voir* clauses. One might then conclude that this argument favors the view that nonstandard inversion is optional, for then (143) is analyzable in the same way as (141a), that is, as having an ordinary finally transitive complement.

Actually, however, sentences like (143a) do not, I think, show anything about the inversion hypothesis or the optionality of nonstandard inversion, for the simple reason that generalization (142) is erroneous. The constraint noted by Kayne is by no means fully general and is possibly specific to the former 1s of passives. For the anaphoric connections in the simple clauses in (144), all incompatible with (142), are entirely well-formed:

(144) a. Ses_i enfants lui_i sont importants.
"Hir's own children are important to hir."
b. Son_i amant semble très beau à $Louise_i$.
"Her own lover seems very handsome to Louise."

c. Sa_i découverte à profité à $Jean\text{-}Claude_i$.
"His own discovery was profitable to Jean-Claude."

d. Son_i ami répondra à $Jacqueline_i$.
"Her own friend will reply to Jacqueline."

Since (142) is false independently of nonstandard sentences, it has no relevant consequences for these, and the well-formedness of (143a) does not impinge on the adequacy of any aspect of the inversion hypothesis.[13]

4.2 Purposive Expressions

One usage of French phrases of the form *pour* + *Infinitive X* translates as English '(in order) to' structures. This is the use referred to as '*pour* + infinitif au sens final' by Sandfeld (1965: 417–42). These cases must be kept distinct from other uses of the same surface expressions.[14] As remarked by Sandfeld (1965: 442), the usage in question is roughly equivalent semantically to the use of *afin de* followed by an infinitive.[15] I refer to such phrases, with the appropriate meanings, as P(URPOSIVE)-PHRASES. Like MAs, P-Phrases are associated with specific nominals, as shown in (145):

(145) Martin a parlé de ses chefs pour amuser Claudine.
"Martin spoke about his bosses in order to amuse Claudine."

In this case, the P-Phrase is clearly linked to *Martin* and not to *ses chefs*. This shows up as a question of which nominal is understood as the (final) 1 of the superficially 1-less infinitive. With 'inherently' reflexive Vs, this association can yield grammaticality contrasts, as in (146):

(146) a. Martin a dit cela de vous pour se/*vous moquer de Louise.
"Martin said that about you in order to make fun of Louise."

b. Le medecin est parti avec nous pour s'/*nous occuper de cela.
"The doctor left with us in order to take care of that."

As observed by Sandfeld (1965: 419), the nominal associated with a P-Phrase must, metaphor aside, be animate.

While there are similarities between the distributions of P-Phrases and MAs, there are also evident differences. In general, as indicated in (114) and (122), MAs are in a clear sense linked to the notion of 1-hood. But this is not necessarily true for P-Phrases, as shown by a variety of cases like those in (147), cited in Sandfeld (1965: 422–23):

(147) a. M. l'abbé—viendra me prendre ici à midi, pour déjeuner avec lui.
"The abbot will come pick me up here at noon, for me to have lunch with him."

b. Notre mère nous appelait aussi pour dire bonjour à M. Mathalène France.
"Our mother called us also in order for us to say hello to Mr. M. France."

c. Elle a donné son enfant à une vielle pour le ramener au pays.
"She gave her child to an old woman in order for her to bring him back home."

So in (147a,b), the P-Phrase is controlled by what appears to be an initial and final 2, while in (147c), the P-Phrase is controlled by what appears to be an initial and final 3. Although many cases parallel to (147) are regarded as marginal at best by my primary consultant, and many cases of control by 2s and 3s seem outright impossible (for reasons about which I have no insight), the general point that P-Phrases can be linked at least in certain cases to nominals with no specifiable connection to 1s does not seem open to challenge.

I do not, however, know of any cases where a P-Phrase cannot be regarded as linked to the head of some initial Term-arc. Beyond (147), this claim is consistent with cases like (145) and (146), in which the controller of the P-Phrase is an initial and final 1. It is also consistent with the fact that P-Phrases can be associated with the earlier 1s of various passives, both plain and reflexive, and both personal and impersonal.

(148) a. un fait qui permet de comprendre le jeu mené par l'Allemagne pour parvenir a ses fins.
"a fact which permits one to understand the game played by Germany in order to reach her goals" Sandfeld (1965: 426)
b. Cela a été dit (par Hervé) pour vous tromper.
"That was said (by Herve) in order to fool you."
c. Cela se dit pour tromper tout le monde.
"That is said to fool everybody."
d. Cela a été fait (par Hervé) pour s'amuser.
"That was done (by Herve) in order to amuse himself."
e. Il a été brutalement mis fin à la discussion par le capitaine (?pour se montrer très fort/s'eclipser plus tôt).
"An end was brutally put to the discussion by the captain (in order to show himself to be very strong/to leave sooner)."

Moreover, the initial term condition is consistent with the fact that P-Phrases are associable with the final 1s of simple unaccusative clauses, since these head initial 2-arcs:

(149) a. Hervé est sorti pour aller chercher des cigarettes.
"Herve went out in order to find some cigarettes."
b. La foule s'est dispersée pour éviter le gaz fumigène.
"The crowd dispersed in order to avoid the tear gas."
c. Marianne est devenue medecin pour aider les pauvres.
"Marianne became a doctor in order to help poor people."

The question arises, then, whether an initial term condition SUFFICES as a specification of the grammatical constraints on P-Phrases. A negative answer is suggested initially by remarks of Zubizarreta (1985: 253n), who claims that in contrast to (150a), the long version of an EXI example like (150b) is ungrammatical:

(150) a. Beaucoup de gens sont venus (pour voir Marie).
"Many people came in order to see Mary."

b. Il est venu beaucoup de gens (*pour voir Marie).
"Many people came (in order to see Mary)."

For speakers having contrasts like (150), an initial term condition does not, evidently, suffice. However, my own principal consultant accepts (150b), as well as other intransitive structures having MAs associated with the EXI pivot.[16] And for her these contrast sharply with *afin de* phrases in this context.[17]

(151) a. Il est parti une femme pour aller chercher des oeufs.
"A woman left in order to go find some eggs."
b. Il est arrivé des irréguliers pour protéger la ville.
"Some irregular troops arrived in order to protect the city."
c. *Il est parti une femme afin d'aller chercher des oeufs.
"A woman left in order to go find some eggs."
d. *Il est arrivé des irréguliers afin de protéger la ville.
"Some irregular troops arrived in order to protect the city."

But even for this speaker, the initial term restriction on P-Phrases does not suffice. This is shown first by the contrast in (152):

(152) a. ?Marcel est le directeur pour aider des gens.
"Marcel is the director in order to help people."
b. *Le directeur, c'est Marcel pour aider des gens.
"The director is Marcel in order to help people."

The compatibility of MAs with both types of predicate nominal construction in (152) (see (104) above) was taken to be allowed because those like (152b) involve P-arc local successors of initial 1-arcs, so that *Marcel* in (152b) would head an initial 1-arc. But then if an initial term condition sufficed for P-Phrases, (152b) would meet it. I conclude that there are further conditions on P-Phrases for all speakers, although these differ for the variants contrasting as to the compatibility of P-Phrases and EXI pivots.

For the variant described by Zubizarreta, one can propose principle (153):

(153) Informal P-Phrase Condition (Stricter Dialect of Zubizarreta 1985)
A P-Phrase in clause C⟨b⟩ is associated with the head of an initial Term-arc A⟨b⟩, and if A is vedette at $c_{initial}$, A has a 1-arc remote local successor which does not have a foundational local successor.

The concept FOUNDATIONAL designates the totality of arcs whose R-sign is a member of the class {P,1,2,3}. Thus (153) imposes two subconditions on the vedette subcase of initial controllers for P-Phrases. The relevant vedette arc must have a 1-arc remote local successor, and the latter arc cannot have a 2-arc, 3-arc or P-arc local successor. This allows the controller to head an initial 1-arc with no local successor, an initial unaccusative 2-arc with a 1-arc local successor, or an initial 1-arc with an 8- or 6-arc local successor. This formulation blocks *(150b), while allowing (150a) and other unaccusative structures, and also blocks *(152b), correctly on the assumption that these are also disallowed for the speakers characterized by Zubizarreta's remarks. Rule (153) would block *(152b) under the analysis suggested earlier for this class of predicate nominal constructions (see (105)) because the initial 1-arc whose head is a potential controller has a P-arc, hence a foundational, local successor.

Principle (153) is, however, too strict for the language of my own primary consultant and other speakers who accept examples like (150b). It can be appropriately weakened by observing the following. While EXI pivots do not, under what I claim is the correct analysis, head 1-arcs, each of them is nonetheless related to a fixed 1-arc in a specific way. Under the analysis in Postal (1986a) illustrated in (34) above, every EXI clause has a relevant structure including the arcs in (154).

(154)

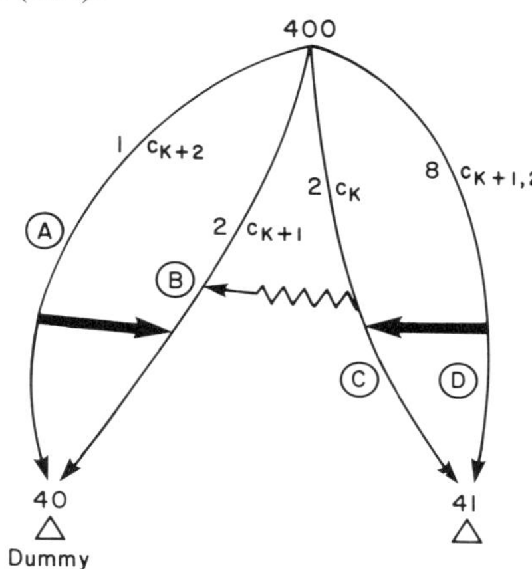

So arc C sponsors B, which in turn has A as a local successor.

It is then straightforward to define a relevant notion 'Realization'. Roughly, Realization is the ancestral of Sponsor, that is, it is Remote Sponsor. 'A is a realization of B' then subsumes 'A is a successor of B' and certain other cases where B remote-sponsors A; see Postal (to appear a, to appear b). Specifically then, in (154), A is a local realization of C. Consequently, one can say the following about P-Phrases. Whereas in the stricter type of French along this dimension, when a P-Phrase is associated with the head of an initial vedette, that arc needs a 1-arc local successor (hence blocking EXI examples in which there is no such successor), in the looser dialect of my principal consultant, the requirement is only that the vedette have a 1-arc local REALIZATION, always provided in EXI structures by the 1-arc local successor (like A in (154)) of the dummy 2-arc. Hence this approach claims that the looser dialect will allow all the initial vedette P-Phrase structures of the stricter one, plus in addition all and only those cases where the vedette-arc has a 1-arc realization (subject to the foundational condition).

(155) Informal P-Phrase Condition (Looser Dialect)
A P-Phrase in clause C⟨b⟩ is associated with the head of an initial Term-arc A⟨b⟩, and if A is vedette at $c_{initial}$, A has a 1-arc local realization which does not have a foundational local successor.

Rule (155) is identical to (153) except that it references 'local realization' instead of 'remote local successor'. No reference to 'remote' is necessary in (155) since the notion Realization itself builds in the ancestral reference designated by 'Remote' affixed to a simpler APG relation between arcs.

Let us consider some further consequences of, and potential problems with, (155), focusing on this rather than on (153), since there are no further data available for the dialect putatively described by (153). First, although it was illustrated in (148) that a P-Phrase can be controlled by the earlier 1 of a passive, none of those examples involved structures in which the earlier 1 appears in a *de* phrase. These were claimed in section 4.2 to instantiate demotion of the earlier 1 to 6 rather than to 8. If this is true, then (155) predicts that this class of phrases should also be possible controllers for P-Phrases in the relevant dialect. While the relevant intuitions seem somewhat problematic, this consequence is probably correct, in view of examples like (156):

(156) a. Le chargement sera accompagné par/de mon frère.
"The load will be accompanied by my brother."
b. Le chargement sera accompagné par/de mon frère pour le protéger.
"The load will be accompanied by my brother in order to protect it."
c. Le pape sera précédé par des gardes/de gardes.
"The pope will be preceded by guards."
d. Le pape sera précédé par des gardes/de gardes pour le protéger.
"The pope will be preceded by guards in order to protect him."

To the extent that these data are correct, P-Phrases thus contrast with MAs with respect to controllability by the heads of 6-arc local successors of 1-arcs. I should note though that at times my consultant has manifested a certain reluctance to accept the variants of (156b,d) containing the preposition *de*. This suggests that there might well be speakers who differentiate the two classes of passives with respect to compatibility with P-Phrases. Such a situation would not require any great changes in the present account. Assuming such speakers shared all other features with the dialect described by rule (155), this difference could be accounted for by positing for them a rule like (157):

(157) Informal P-Phrase Condition (Conceivable But As Yet Unattested Dialect)
A P-Phrase in clause C⟨b⟩ is associated with the head of an initial Term-arc A⟨b⟩, and if A is vedette at $c_{initial}$, A has a 1-arc local realization which does not have a non–8-arc local successor.

Rule (157) is identical to (155) except that the possible local successors of the

1-arc realization are limited by the predicate non–8-arc rather than by the predicate Foundational.

Next one should ask whether (155) is consistent with an important fact. In contrast to MAs, P-Phrases are compatible with the unique Vs *voici* and *voilà* in contexts like (158) and (159).[18]

(158) a. Voici Hervé (*à regret) chez ses parents.
"Here is Herve (with regret) at his parents' place."
b. La voilà (*avec enthousiasme) pour vous aider.
"There she is (with enthusiasm) in order to help you."

If one refers to the postverbal nominals with these Vs as *V Pivots,* (158b) and (159a,b) show the compatibility of V pivots with P-Phrases.

(159) a. Voici Hervé pour vous aider.
"Herve is here in order to help you."
b. La voilà pour nous conduire en ville.
"There she is in order to drive us to town."

There is every reason to assume that V pivots head final 2-arcs, since this predicts their postverbal word order and the possibility of their determining accusative PCs, as in (158b) and (159b). One could then simply assume that V pivots also head initial 2-arcs, satisfying the initial term requirement for P-Phrases. If they only head such 2-arcs, then it is properly predicted by rule (122) that V pivots are incompatible with MAs. But it is then WRONGLY entailed by (155) that they are incompatible with P-Phrases.

Suppose, though, that the structure of clause (160a) is (160b).

(160) a. Voilà Hervé.
"There's Herve."
b.

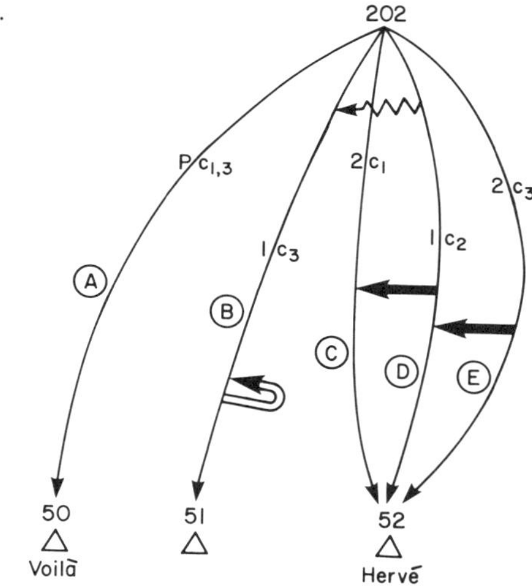

This structure takes clauses containing such instances of *voilà* to be initially unaccusative, represented by the initial 2-arc C. As is common, this has a 1-arc local successor, D. But it is claimed that, uniquely, the noninitial 1 of these odd Vs determines a dummy 1, invisible because of the obligatory self-erasure of the dummy 1-arc, B. To preserve stratal uniqueness, the 1-arc local successor, D, itself needs a local successor, here E, which is claimed to be a 2-arc, to account for the final 2 status of the initial 2.

The suggested analysis has the following properties. Although *Hervé* in (160b) heads a first 1-arc and an initial vedette, it is still properly incompatible with MAs. For rule (122) requires the associated nominal to head a remote local successor of a strict acting 1-arc. But *Hervé* does not, since D in (160b) is NOT a strict acting 1-arc or even an acting 1-arc. This follows since its local successor, E, is a 2-arc. However, the initial arc headed by *Hervé* does have a local realization which is a 1-arc, namely, B, and one which does not have a foundational local successor, since B has no local successor at all. Although D is also a 1-arc local realization of C, this cannot suffice to permit association with a P-Phrase, since D's local successor, a 2-arc, is foundational. Therefore (155) claims that only arc B in (160b) can license the presence of a P-Phrase associated with *Hervé*. Note that given the analysis in (160b), it would be predicted by rule (153) that V pivots are incompatible with P-Phrases in the STRICTER dialect. For D cannot license a P-Phrase, since its local successor is a 2-arc. Since Zubizarreta provides no information about examples like (159), I cannot presently evaluate the correctness of this claim.

While it might be granted that an analysis like (160b) interacts with rules (122) and (155) to make correct predictions, (160b) certainly has features capable of generating scepticism, in particular, the presence of a 1-arc which obligatorily self-erases, obligatorily since no *voilà* or *voici* clause ever contains a surface 1. However, the representation in (160b) of a dummy 1-arc, invisible because of self-erasure, can, I think (contra Morin 1985), be supported by the presence of the nominative PC in cases like (161b). The argument depends on a parallelism between (161a,b) and e.g. (161c,d).

(161) a. Voilà Marie prisonnière de ses mensonges.
"Marie is a prisoner of her lies."
b. Ne voilà-t-il pas Marie prisonnière de ses mensonges?
"Isn't Marie a prisoner of her lies?"
c. Il pleut.
"It rains."
d. Ne pleut-il pas?
"Isn't it raining?"

The idea is that the dummy posited with the Vs *voici* and *voilà* is obligatorily invisible except in the 'inverted PC' cases with the latter. This kind of distinction in invisibility is independently attestable in French, namely, with the

V *falloir.* Colloquial French allows either of the declaratives in (162a,b). But while (162c) is a possible interrogative, (162d) (as an interrogative) is ill-formed.

(162) a. Il faut partir.
"It is necessary to leave."
b. Faut partir.
"It is necessary to leave."
c. Faut-il partir?
"Is it necessary to leave?"
d. *Faut partir?
"Is it necessary to leave?"

In short, the dummy nominal associated with *falloir* can be invisible only when it determines a proclitic.

The structure in (160b) is further motivated by the fact, discussed in Kayne (1983) and Morin (1985), that under certain conditions, the V pivot of *voilà* can determine a kind of agreement. Thus, in addition to (163a), many variants of colloquial French allow (163b), and some may only allow the latter:

(163) a. Ne la voilà-t-il pas prisonnière de ses mensonges?
"Isn't she a prisoner of her lies?"
b. Ne la voilà-t-elle pas prisonnière de ses mensonges?
"Isn't she a prisoner of her lies?"

And besides (164a), these same variants allow (164b).[19]

(164) a. Les conditions nécessaires, ne les voilà-t-il pas réunies?
"Are not the necessary conditions found there?"
b. Les conditions nécessaires, ne les voilà-t-elles pas réunies?
"Are not the necessary conditions found there?"

The argument here is that given a structure like (160b), the agreement of the nominative PC in (163b) and (164b) with the accusative PC representing the final 2 reduces to an independently attested phenomenon, that called 'brother-in-law' agreement in RG work.[20] This phenomenon has recently been subsumed under a general theory of agreement in Aissen (to appear).

The idea is that in certain cases, the features relevant for agreement can be 'passed' from the head of an arc A to an arc B. The theory limits this kind of feature 'passing' to structures in which A and B are related in a fixed way, namely, B must OVERRUN A. Roughly (see Johnson and Postal 1980: 274), as indicated at the end of section 3.1, C overruns D when they are neighbors, they have the same (Term) R-sign, and C's first coordinate index is +1 of D's last coordinate index. One instance of these conditions is the case where B is a dummy arc locally sponsored by A and having the same (Nuclear Term) R-sign as A. This subcase is illustrated by the phenomenon seen in English *there* sentences like (165):

(165) a. There is/seems to be a gorilla in that box.
b. There are/seem to be gorillas in that box.

The point is then that the 1-arcs B and D in (160b) satisfy the conditions for brother-in-law feature passing and hence brother-in-law agreement, because B overruns D. But evidently this state of affairs holds ONLY because of the postulation of just those features of (160b) that are controversial, namely, the 1-arc local successor D and the self-erasing dummy 1-arc A. Given these, one can account for the unique properties of (163b) and (164b) by assuming that French allows, though only in extraordinarily restricted environments, feature passing in gender and number between the head of a V pivot and the head of the dummy arc sponsored by the 1-arc (local successor) that the former heads. This will determine a feminine singular nominative PC *-elle* in (163b) and a feminine plural (though only orthographically) PC *-elles* in (164b) by the regular mechanisms, whatever these are, determining agreement between the PC and the final 1 in cases like (166).[21]

(166) a. Ta mère est-elle/*-il malade?
"Is your mother sick?"
b. Ton père est-il/*-elle malade?
"Is your father sick?"
c. Quand ta mère a-t-elle/*-il crié?
"When did your mother cry out?"
d. Quand ton père a-t-il/*-elle criè?
"When did your father cry out?"

Consequently, under the analysis in (160b), the agreement in cases like (163b) and (164b) is reduced to familiar terms in two independent senses. First, postulation of the 1-arcs in (160b) reduces the agreement in these sentences to the same agreement found in (166), which is uncontroversially agreement with a final 1. Secondly, the same analysis subsumes the agreement in (163b) and (164b) under the agreement theory, more precisely, the feature-passing aspect of that theory, worked out in Aissen (to appear). Without a structure including the controversial 1-arcs in (160b), the agreements in these sentences remain a phenomenon absolutely unique for French, in which a nominative PC agrees with an accusative PC.[22] I conclude that these considerations render plausible the view that, because of the existence in clauses with V pivots of arcs like B and D in (160b), the compatibility of V pivots with P-Phrases is properly consistent with rule (155).[23]

Continuing to explore the consequences of (155), we observe next that in the looser dialect, P-Phrases also contrast with MAs with respect to possible association with the postverbal nominal in *Il y a* constructions. Call these nominals *Ya Pivots:*

(167) a. Il y a une armée pour nous protéger.
"There is an army in order to protect us."
b. *Il y a une armée à regret.
"There is an army with regret."

(168) a. Il y a des policiers pour combattre le crime.
"There are policemen in order to fight crime."
b. *Il y a des policiers avec enthousiasme.
"There are policemen with enthusiasm."

These facts will follow from assumptions already elaborated, in particular, rules (122) and (155) for MAs and P-Phrases, respectively, if such examples have a partial structure like (169) for (167a).

(169)

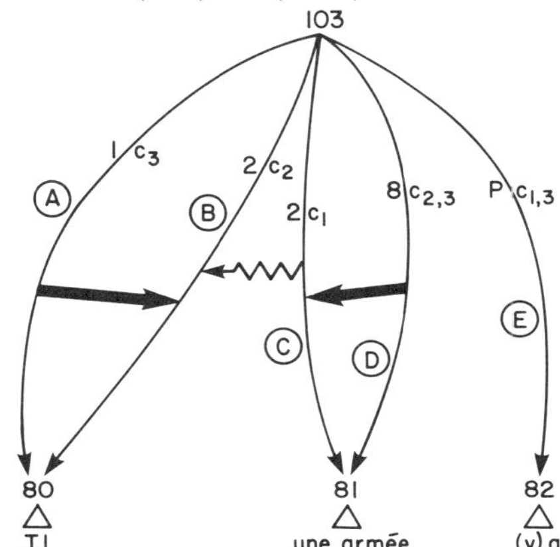

This structure blocks MAs because the vedette-arc C does not have a remote local successor which is a strict acting 1-arc, since it has no 1-arc remote local successor at all. On the other hand, C does have a 1-arc local realization, A, which has no local successor, satisfying all aspects of the looser dialect P-Phrase condition in (155). It is, of course, predicted from rule (153) that P-Phrases are incompatible with Ya pivots in the stricter dialect, a matter about which Zubizarreta (1985) again provides no information.

Assuming, then, that something like (155) is correct for P-Phrases in the looser dialect, this rule implies that P-Phrases cannot be associated with MOST inversion 3s, since an inversion 3 heads an initial 1-arc with a 3-arc, hence not 8-arc, local successor. There is only one exception. A P-Phrase will satisfy (155) and thus be compatible with an inversion 3 IF the 1-arc local predecessor of the relevant inversion 3-arc has a 1-arc realization. Specifically, compatibility is predicted in cases of IMPERSONAL inversion, where the 1-arc local predecessor of the inversion 3-arc locally sponsors a dummy 1-arc. This type of inversion has not yet been discussed. But cases which are, I believe, properly analyzed as instantiations of this pattern exist in French, namely, with the V *falloir*.

(170) a. Marc a besoin d'une voiture pour transporter ces livres.
"Marc needs a car in order to transport these books."
b. Cette voiture, il la lui faut pour transporter ces livres.
"Hir needs this car in order to transport these books."

Forms like (170b) are allowed by (155) under the assumption that such clauses have structure including the representation in (171); see Postal (1986a: chapter 3) for an argument for this representation, in particular, for the claim that the final 3 heads an earlier 1-arc.

(171)

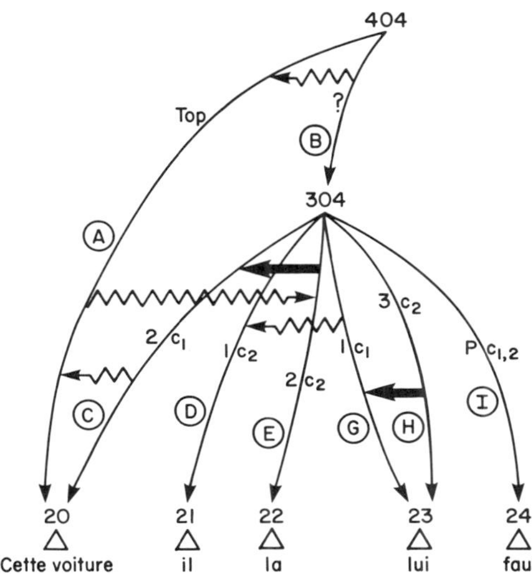

Here D satisfies the requirement of a 1-arc local realization having no non-8-arc local successor. Note though that rule (153) would block a structure like (171) and thus predicts that examples like (170b) are ill-formed in the stricter dialect, a claim again not testable on the basis of Zubizarreta (1985).

What (155) precludes, however, is control of a P-Phrase by an inversion 3 in a PERSONAL inversion structure, that is, in which some other nominal advances to 1. For in that case the 1-arc local realization condition is not met. It is difficult to get relevant information about P-Phrases in non-CIC personal inversion cases, since they cannot with semantic naturalness be associated with the kind of independent clauses, like (105b), (106b), (107b), or (110), which one can suspect of being inversion clauses. That is, since e.g. (172a) is already anomalous at best, the ill-formedness of (172b) cannot be taken to show anything much.

(172) a. ??Le sadique a bénéficié de sa souffrance pour vous choquer.
"The sadist benefited from hir's suffering in order to shock you."
b. * Sa souffrance a bénéficié au sadique pour vous choquer.
"The sadist benefited from hir's suffering in order to shock you."

Thus the only available test of the claim of (155) that personal inversion is incompatible with P-Phrases currently has to be drawn from the CIC under the hypothesis that nonstandard CIC complements (can) involve inversion.

The key property of (155) for current purposes is the following. It allows an initial 1-arc which is a final 1-arc to be a controller of a P-Phrase. Therefore it predicts that the head of the kind of French 1-arc launcher which has a 3-arc postimage can be a controller. But (155) will not allow the head of an inversion 3-arc launcher to be a controller unless it is a case of impersonal inversion. Therefore, if it could be argued that IMPERSONAL inversion is impossible in CIC complements, (155) would interact with the inversion hypothesis to predict clear contrasts in the behavior of CIC complements with standard and nonstandard Vs.

Moreover, there are grounds to conclude that impersonal inversion is NOT possible in CIC complements. First, the V *falloir* which, under the present analysis, only occurs in impersonal inversion clauses, cannot be the main V of a CIC complement:[24]

(173) a. *Cela (le) (lui) a fait falloir une voiture.
"That made hir need a car."
b. *Ces évenements (le) (lui) ont fait falloir des gardes.
"These events made hir need guards."
c. *Ceci pourrait (le) (lui) faire falloir partir.
"This could make hir need to leave."

Suppose one defines the notion *Prelauncher* as an arc which is a neighbor of a P-arc predecessor of a U-arc. Every clausal arc in a CU complement is thus a prelauncher regardless of whether it is a launcher. The simplest and hence a priori most desirable account of facts like those exemplified in *(173a,b,c) would just block all dummy-arc prelaunchers, as in (174):[25]

(174) If A is a prelauncher, then A is not a dummy arc.

Principle (174) would predict, correctly, that impersonal clauses like those in (175a,b) cannot be embedded as CIC complements:

(175) a. Il semble qu'Hervé est stupide.
"It seems that Herve is stupid."
b. Il paraît que cette voiture a été volée.
"It appears that that car was stolen."
c. *Cela (le) (lui) fait sembler qu'Hervé est stupide.
"That makes it seem (to hir) that Herve is stupid."
d. *Cela (le) (lui) fait paraître que cette voiture a été volée.
"That makes it appear (to hir) that that car was stolen."

Actually, a refinement is necessary for the case where an ill-formed structure like e.g. *(175d) contains no accusative PC. A priori, as a reader observes, that structure could have an analysis in which the complement clause is an initial and final 2, there being no final 1 at all, as allowed by our earlier assumptions. However, this possibility would seem to be independently excluded by the fact that the complement with Vs like *paraître* and *sembler* otherwise only occurs in association with a dummy. I take this to be a function of OBLIGATORY (object) extraposition with these Vs, yielding a dummy 2 which advances to 1. This constraint is independently motivated, since it blocks such otherwise potentially grammatical structures as (176a); compare (176b):

(176) a. *Qu'il est/soit stupide me semble.
"That he is stupid seems to me."
b. Qu'il est/soit stupide est évident.
"That he is stupid is evident."

Further, (174) predicts correctly that impersonal clauses with Vs like *incomber,* which only occurs impersonally in independent clauses, and *tarder,* which can occur impersonally, are also not embeddable as CIC complements.

(177) a. Il m'incombe de le faire.
"It is incumbent on me to do it."
b. *Cela (me) (le) fait incomber de le faire.
"That made it incumbent on me to do it."
c. Il me tarde de la voir.
"I am anxious to see her."
d. *Son charme (me) (l') a fait tarder de la voir.
"Her charm made me anxious to see her."

In addition, (174) predicts that EXI clauses cannot be CIC complements. I believe this is also correct, even though for most EXI cases it is hard to show it. For example, given (178a,b), it is not clear that (178c) is not ambiguously a correspondent of the latter as well as of the former:

(178) a. un avocat sortira.
"A lawyer will go out."
b. Il sortira un avocat.
"A lawyer will go out."
c. Cela fera sortir un avocat.
"That will make a lawyer go out."

For independent French principles would guarantee that even if clauses like (178b) were embedded, the dummy would not be visible in the main clause. This holds since dummy 2s are uniformly invisible in French.[26]

Nonetheless, there is evidence that EXI clauses are not embeddable, based on the unique V *suffire,* mentioned earlier. This has the property of requiring its EXI pivot to be marked with the preposition *de.* Therefore, if EXI clauses are embeddable, one would expect that a nominal marked with *de* would be possible in a CIC complement with this V. For my consultant, this V does not embed very happily in the CIC. Nonetheless, if it is embedded, it is quite clear that no marking with *de* is possible.

(179) a. Une voiture (me) suffit.
"One car is sufficient for me."
b. Il (me) suffit d'/*∅ une voiture.
"One car is sufficient for me."

c. ?Cela (m') a fait suffire une voiture.
"That made one car be sufficient (for me)."
d. *Cela (m') a fait suffire d'une voiture.
"That made one car be sufficient (for me)."

The only possibility at best is that in which the relevant CIC nominal behaves like a complement final 1 and does NOT behave like an EXI pivot.

The proposal to ban all dummy-arc prelaunchers is thus attractive. Nonetheless, it is problematic, in view of the fact that at least two types of structures which require dummies in independent clauses CAN be embedded in the CIC. These are *il y a* structures and weather expressions.

(180) a. Il y a des guerres en Afrique.
"There are wars in Africa."
b. Il pleut.
"It rains."
c. Pourquoi Dieu a-t-il laissé y avoir des guerres en Afrique?
"Why has God let there be wars in Africa?"
d. Dieu peut faire pleuvoir.
"God can make it rain."

It is not clear how to distinguish these structures from those which are properly blocked by (174). One proposal would be to weaken (174) so that it only blocks those prelauncher cases in which there is a dummy 1-arc which is not a local successor, or equivalently, in the framework of Johnson and Postal (1980), to block prelauncher 1-arc GHOSTS.[27] This works all right, except that it does not provide a basis for the incompatibility of EXI sentences and CIC complements, since under my analysis (see (34)), these involve 2-arc ghosts. However, there is some reason to believe this is not a serious problem and that it is correct to weaken (174) to (181):

(181) If A is a 1-arc prelauncher, then A is not a ghost arc.

As it stands, (181) will block *(173a,b,c), *(175c,d), and *(177b), on the plausible assumption that all these inherently involve 1-arc ghosts. It does not, however, block e.g. *(179d) and thus offers no insight into the contrast between this and e.g. (180c,d). But Rouveret and Vergnaud (1980: 148–49n) observe that there is, entirely independently of the CIC, a constraint precluding EXI structures but, notably, not weather-V structures, in contexts where no explicit dummy can appear. Hence they cite such contrasts as (182):

(182) a. Ici, il tombe rarement beaucoup de neige sans pleuvoir.
"Here, lots of snow rarely falls without it raining."
b. *Ici, il pleut rarement sans tomber beaucoup de neige.
"Here, it rarely rains without lots of snow falling."

In (182a), the EXI structure occurs in the finite main clause in association with an explicit dummy. But in the ungrammatical (182b), the EXI structure must appear in the nonfinite constituent, and without any visible dummy. Similar contrasts are found with *il y a* constructions in the same environment:

(183) a. Il peut arriver des sinistres sans y avoir de morts.
"There can be disasters without there being any deaths."
b. *Il peut y avoir des morts sans arriver de sinistres.
"There can be deaths without there being any disasters."

It seems clear then that there is some constraint, although one I will not try to give any analysis of, which allows both weather expressions and *il y a* expressions in infinitives but which blocks EXI structures in these. This being the case, there is no reason to reject (181) simply because it fails to block *(179d), since there is good reason to assume that the latter would be blocked by the constraint motivated independently of the CIC which must exclude *(182b) and *(183b).

Implicit in the immediately preceding discussion is the assumption that something blocks EXI constructions from taking advantage of the freedom allowed by the nonrelevance of the Final 1-Arc Law for CU complements. This freedom would a priori allow an EXI structure as CIC complement to satisfy (181) simply by not having a 1-arc local successor for the dummy 2-arc defining this construction. But this is apparently precluded by the constraint operative in (182) and (183).

To finish the discussion of the possibility of impersonal inversion in CIC complements, I conclude that there seems to be ground for the view that a principle like (181) or something with similar entailments excludes all GHOST 1-arc prelaunchers. This being so, inversion in CIC complements must be either personal or absolute. But the initial vedettes of both these types of inversion clause are claimed by rule (155) to be incompatible with P-Phrases, for the 1-arc realization condition in this principle can then not be satisfied. Thus (155) interacts with the inversion hypothesis to predict the existence of contrasts in the associability with P-Phrases of apparent final 1s in standard and nonstandard sentences.

Testing these predictions about the distribution of P-Phrases in CIC structures is complicated by the fact that such embedding is perhaps not entirely natural. Nonetheless, certain facts seem reasonably clear. When a standard CIC sentence with a transitive complement contains a P-Phrase, this can be associated with the main clause 3 (complement final 1), in accord with (155).

(184) a. On lui a fait faire cela pour les soulager.
"One had him do that in order to give them relief."
b. Marianne leur a fait acheter cela pour réparer les dégats.
"Marianne made them buy that in order to repair the damages."
c. Cela lui a fait trahir ses amis pour éviter de se faire condamner.
"That made hir betray hir's friends in order to avoid getting condemned."

So the P-Phrase in (184a) is understandable ambiguously as associated either with the main clause initial and final 1 manifested as *on* or with the complement initial and final 1 represented by the PC *lui*. Either of these forms can be understood as the 1 of *(les) soulager*. The association with *lui* is compatible with (155) on the standard transitive analysis, in which the nominal underlying this PC is both the initial and the final 1 of the complement. Similarly, in (184b) either the main-clause-initial and -final 1 *Marianne* of the complement-final 1 represented as the PC *leur* can be the controller of *réparer*. In (184c), association with *lui* is the only possibility, because of the inanimate character of the main clause 1. In cases like (185), it is the reflexive agreement facts which guarantee that the purposive can ONLY be associated with COMPLEMENT-final 1.

(185) a. J'ai laissé faire cela à Hervé pour se rattraper.
"I let Herve do that in order to make up (for something)."
b. J'ai laissé lire cela à Louis pour s'instruire.
"I let Louis read that in order to educate himself."[28]

Recalling the conclusion of section 4.1 that CIC inversion is in general only optional, the inversion hypothesis will then combine with rule (155) to make certain predictions about nonstandard CIC sentences. One is that in all those which are, as a result of independent constraints like FC, ONLY analyzable as inversion structures, the apparent complement-final 1, which is the initial 1, but which is, according to this hypothesis, a FINAL 3, should not be associable with a P-Phrase, in spite of facts like those illustrated in (184) and (185). This claim follows from the 1-arc local realization condition in combination with the conclusion that CIC inversion cannot be impersonal, that is, cannot be associated with a dummy 1-arc realization of the 1-arc with a 3-arc local successor. Significantly, this incompatibility seems to be manifested in the data.

(186) a. Le medecin vous verra pour vous soulager.
"The doctor will see you in order to give you relief."
b. On vous fera voir au medecin pour vous soulager.
"One will have the doctor see you in order to give you relief."
c. Cela nous a fait voir au medecin (*pour s'amuser).
"That made the doctor see us in order to amuse himself."
d. Je vous ferai voir au medecin pour m'/*s'amuser.
"I will have the doctor see you in order to amuse myself."

It appears that it is impossible in (186b) to associate the purposive with *(au) medecin,* despite the impetus in this direction from the reality that it is natural for doctors to relieve people.[29] Expectably then, (186c,d), which lack any legal controllers for their P-Phrases, are ungrammatical when the P-Phrase 1 must be third person. Although inversion is optional with *voir,* FC determines that the only analysis of examples like (186b,c,d) with a chance of grammaticality are inversion structures. But when a P-Phrase is present, these are incompatible with rule (155).

Similar correct predictions of incompatibilities between nonstandard Vs and P-Phrases are seen in (187):

(187) a. Le témoin vous a reconnu pour aider la police/se disculper.
"The witness recognized you in order to aid the police/show himself to be innocent."
b. Nous vous avons fait reconnaître au témoin pour *se/nous disculper.
"We had you recognized by the witness to show himself/ourselves to be innocent."

One could also cite examples parallel to (186b,c,d) and (187b) with *connaître,* e.g. (188b,c).

(188) a. ??Joanne vous connaîtra pour se distraire.
"Joanne will know you in order to amuse herself."
b. Je vous ferai connaître à Joanne pour me/*se distraire.
"I will have Joanne know (meet) you in order to amuse myself."
c. Cela m'a fait connaître à Joanne (*pour avancer sa carrière).
"That made Joanne know (meet) me (in order to advance her career)."

However, as a reader observes, it is doubtful whether these support the inversion hypothesis, since there is a constraint on combining stative readings of *connaître* with the P-Phrases illustrated in (188a), even in non=CIC cases, and this could block (188b,c) independently of the considerations of this monograph. However, this is not really relevant, since there is no analogue of (188a) for either *voir* or *reconnaître,* and thus (186) and (187) support the hypothesis at issue here. That is, as the inversion hypothesis predicts, the nominal heading the main clause 3-arc in nonstandard sentences does not, unlike the parallel nominal in standard CIC sentences, behave like a final 1 of the complement. Rather, with respect to condition (155) applied to the embedded clause, it behaves like an inversion 3, more precisely an inversion 3 not associated with a dummy 1-arc realization of the initial 1-arc.

Consequently the facts of P-Phrase distribution, as well as those of MA distribution, reveal further anomalies if (all) nonstandard CIC sentences are treated as having standard transitive complements. But these exceptions vanish under the inversion analysis of nonstandard sentences.

4.3 Phrases with *sans*

An argument in favor of the inversion hypothesis similar to those in sections 4.1 and 4.2 can be based on the distribution of expressions of the form *sans* + infinitive, which correspond semantically to English phrases of the type ⟨*without* V + ing X⟩. I refer to the relevant phrases as *S(ans)*-Phrases. Typical examples include (189a,b):

(189) a. La bonne a répondu sans m'en avertir.
"The maid replied without informing me of it."
b. Marie-Louise a été arrêtée (par la police) sans protester.
"Marie-Louise was arrested (by the police) without protesting."

While S-Phrases, like MAs, seem in some sense linked to 1s, the conditions on their distribution are rather different from those arrived at in section 4.1 for that adverbial type. This is already shown by (189). For while the S-Phrase in (189a) is associated with the initial (hence first) and also final 1, that in (189b) is associated with the final 1 of a passive, which is not the first 1 and which does not correspond to the head of an initial vedette arc.

Moreover, it cannot be claimed that the linkage between the S-Phrase and the final 1 in (189b) is due to the fact that this is an initial 2. For (190a) shows that initial 2s which are final 2s cannot control S-Phrases, and (190b,c,d) suggest that the nominal associated with an S-Phrase in clause C⟨b⟩ need not head an initial arc with tail ⟨b⟩:

(190) a. La police a arrêté Marie-Louise sans protester.
"The police arrested Marie-Louise without protesting."
b. Jacqueline est difficile à supporter sans le savoir.
"Jacqueline is difficult to bear without knowing it."
c. Jacqueline a été prouvée coupable sans s'en rendre compte.
"Jacqueline was proved guilty without realizing it."
d. Jacqueline s'est fait casser le bras sans porter plainte.
"Jacqueline got her arm broken without filing a complaint."

In (190b), there is a case to be made that the main clause final 1 is not an initial constituent of the main clause but only an initial 2 of the *supporter* clause. The main clause status is then due to so-called 'object raising'; see Fauconnier (1974: chapter 4), Ruwet (1982: chapter 2), and Legendre (1986). In (190c), the main clause final 1 is arguably not an initial 2 of the main clause but only an initial 1 of the adjectival complement. Its main clause status would be due to the restricted sort of raising of complement 1s to main clause 2s allowed in French. Finally, in (190d) the main clause final 1 is arguably an initial possessor of the body-part noun which is the head of the complement 2. It owes its clausal status as a 3 to the sort of raising referred to in the RG literature as Possessor Ascension.[30] If even one of these analyses is correct in essence, an S-Phrase in a clause C need not be associated with the head of an INITIAL arc in C. The linkages in (189b) and (190b,c,d) also differentiate the distribution of S-Phrases from that of P-Phrases, which do seem to require an initial arc condition and which do not in general associate with the final 1s of passives.

On the basis of the cases cited so far, one might assume that an S-Phrase in a clause C must simply be associated with the FINAL 1 of C. This is consistent with the further fact that S-Phrases can be associated with the final 1s of either unergative or unaccusative intransitives and with those of the kind of underlying transitive structures claimed earlier to involve antipassivization.

(191) a. Hervé a écrit à sa mère sans lui dire son adresse.
"Herve wrote to his mother without telling her his address."

b. Hervé est sorti sans laisser un message pour vous.
"Herve went out without leaving a message for you."
c. Hervé a mangé sans parler.
"Herve ate without speaking."
d. Hervé s'est décrit sans omettre ses fautes.
"Herve described himself without omitting his faults."

But this condition is too strong, since S-Phrases can also be associated with the underlying 1s of passives, both plain and reflexive, both personal and impersonal, and regardless of whether the relevant underlying 1 is manifested as a visible surface form.[31]

(192) a. Ces tortures doivent être subies sans protester.
"These tortures must be endured without protesting."
b. Cela devrait être fait sans en avertir personne.
"That should be done without informing anyone of it."
c. Les tortures, ça se subit sans broncher.
"Tortures are endured without flinching." (Ruwet 1972: 98 n)
d. Il devrait être mis fin à cette grève (par le gouvernement) sans donner une occasion aux communistes.
"An end must be brought to this strike (by the government) without giving an opportunity to the Communists."
e. Cela a été proposé par Louise sans m'en avertir.
"That was proposed by Louise without informing me about it."

It might then seem that a condition on an S-Phrase in clause C is simply that it be associated with the head of SOME 1-arc in C, as in (193):

(193) Informal Constraint on S-Phrases (First Version)
An S-Phrase in a clause C⟨b⟩ must be associated with the head of some 1-arc A⟨b⟩.

Under assumptions about EXI already discussed, e.g., that an EXI pivot heads no 1-arc, (193) would properly predict the incompatibility of S-Phrases and EXI pivots, noted in Ruwet (1982):

(194) a. Une femme est arrivée sans me prévenir.
"A woman arrived without informing me."
b. *Il est arrivé une femme sans me prévenir.
"A woman arrived without informing me."
c. Trois accusés ont été condamnés sans savoir pourquoi.
"Three accused persons were convicted without knowing why." (Ruwet 1982: 288)
d. Il a été condamné trois accusés (*sans savoir pourquoi).
"Three accused persons were convicted (without knowing why)." (Ruwet 1982: 288)

And a slight extension (see (197)) can also be made to predict that, in sharp contrast to the situation with P-Phrases (in the looser dialect), S-Phrases CANNOT be linked with either V pivots or Ya pivots:

(195) a. Voici Hervé (*sans savoir pourquoi).
"Here is Herve (without knowing why)."
b. Voilà le medecin (*sans vouloir y être).
"There's the doctor (without wanting to be there)."
c. Il y a un gorille dans ce placard (*sans vouloir y être).
"There is a gorilla in this closet (without wanting to be there)."

However, (193) seems too loose, for it fails to predict that, like P-Phrases, S-Phrases are compatible only with the least-complex type of predicate nominal construction, as shown in (196):[32]

(196) a. Je suis le directeur sans vouloir l'être.
"I am the director without wanting to be."
b. Le directeur, c'est moi (*sans vouloir l'être).
"The director is me (without wanting to be)."

The discussion of MAs in section 4.2 concluded that predicate nominal constructions like (196b) had an analysis under which the predicate nominal is an earlier 1. If this is correct, then (193) would not block the ungrammatical long form of (196b). For this would involve an S-Phrase controlled by the head of a P-arc local successor of a 1-arc, satisfying (193). In the case of parallel facts with P-Phrases, I proposed a constraint on the (remote) local successors of the initial arcs, which had to be nonfoundational. A similar move is possible here, strengthening (193) to (197):

(197) Informal Constraint on S-Phrases (Final Version)
An S-Phrase in clause C⟨b⟩ must be associated with the head of some 1-arc A⟨b⟩ which has no foundational local successor.

Under the analysis of predicate nominals mentioned earlier, *(196b) is ungrammatical because its initial 1-arc has a P-arc, hence a foundational, local successor; thus only the first part of the condition in (197) can be satisfied by *moi* with respect to the S-Phrase.[33] Note that, unlike (193), (197) blocks the association of S-Phrases with V pivots. For even though, under the analysis in section 4.2, V pivots head 1-arc local successors of initial unaccusative 2-arcs, those 1-arcs have 2-arc—hence foundational—local successors, violating (197).

However, as required, (197) is consistent with cases like (192d,e), where the S-Phrase is controlled by the passive 8, since that heads an 8-arc local successor of the (initial) 1-arc. If rule (197) is the basic constraint on S-Phrase distribution, S-Phrases should also be compatible with those earlier passive 1s which are marked, not with *par,* but with *de.* Since these were taken to involve demotion to 6, they also satisfy the requirement of a nonfoundational local successor, because a 6-arc is not foundational.

(198) a. Mon père a accompagné le chargement précieux sans le regretter/savoir pourquoi/le révéler.
"My father accompanied the precious load without regretting it/knowing why/revealing it."

b. Le chargement précieux a été accompagné par/de mon père sans le regretter/savoir pourquoi/le révéler.
"The precious load was accompanied by my father without regretting it/knowing why/revealing it."

(199) a. Les soldats ont obéi aux ordres sans les approuver.
"The soldiers obeyed the orders without approving them."

b. Les ordres ont été obéis par les/des soldats sans les approuver.
"The orders were obeyed by the soldiers without approving them."

As with control of P-Phrases by this kind of *de* phrase, however, it appears that at times there is some reluctance to accept their control of S-Phrases. Possibly then, there is a variant of French which limits S-Phrases more narrowly, allowing the local successor of the relevant 1-arc only to be an 8-arc.

Sandfeld (1965: 503) gives an example which he interprets in a way which would be incompatible with (197):

(200) Trois jours avaient suffi à Mlle. Ferray, sans se remuer beaucoup, pour découvrir . . . .
"Three days were sufficient for Mademoiselle Ferray, without engaging in much activity, to discover . . . ."

The implication is that the S-Phrase in (200) is associated with the 3 *Mlle. Ferray.* Were this the case, (197) could not be satisfied even if the main clause of (200) were an inversion structure and the final 3 headed an earlier 1-arc. However, Sandfeld's analysis is clearly a mistake. For it entails that the S-Phrase modifies the V *suffi,* when it really modifies *découvrir.* That is, (200) means 'Three days were sufficient for Mlle. Ferray to do something, namely, to discover . . . without going to much trouble'. I conclude that in (200) the S-Phrase has been 'extracted' from the *pour* phrase, and is associated, in accord with (197), with the final 1 of the latter clause. It just happens that there is a further 'control' relation between the 3 of the *suffire* clause and the final 1 of the *pour* phrase. Note, incidentally, that the particular *pour* phrase in (200) is NOT a P-Phrase and that the fact that it is controlled by a 3 has no relevance for the discussion in section 4.2. Sandfeld (1965: 501) himself gives examples which show that S-Phrases are 'extractable', e.g. (201):

(201) Sans être exactement les mêmes partout, on constate que les règles relatives à la position des mots obéissent à des tendances dominantes.
"Without being exactly the same everywhere, one notes that the rules relevant to the position of words obey prevailing tendencies."

Here, although superficially external to it, the sentence-initial S-Phrase is associated with the complement of *constate,* that is, it really modifies *obéissent.* Hence the apparent association of the S-Phrase with the 3 in (200) is due to the fact, independent of the S-Phrase, that the 3 controls the final 1 of the *pour* phrase.

While S-Phrase 'extractability' raises no difficulty of principle, it does reveal a clear weakness of the informal formulation in (197). For this speaks about 'clause' when the 'extractability' facts show that the real constraint involving 1-hood is at best on clauses in which an S-Phrase appears in a constituent INDEPENDENTLY of 'extraction'. In APG terms, the constraint would presumably refer to an arc A headed by an S-Phrase where A is not a successor, or possibly, not an Overlay arc successor, Overlay arcs being those headed by the nominals raised in such cases as topicalization, questioning, etc.; see Johnson and Postal (1980: chapter 7, section 6).

If we ignore such issues, which are peripheral to current concerns, the relevant consequence for the inversion hypothesis is that (197) entails that S-Phrases CANNOT be associated with inversion 3s, which by definition correspond to the heads of 1-arcs having 3-arc—hence foundational—local successors. And this seems correct in simple inversion clauses, both personal and impersonal.

(202) a. J'ai eu cette idée sans m'en rendre compte.
"I had that idea without realizing it."
b. Cette idée m'est venue (*sans m'en rendre compte).
"That idea came to me (without realizing it)."
c. Nous avons cru le gouvernment corrumpu sans en parler à personne.
"We believed the government corrupt without speaking about it to anyone."
d. Le gouvernement nous a semblé corrumpu (*sans en parler à personne).
"The government seemed corrupt to us (without speaking about it to anyone)."
e. Hervé a une vielle bagnole sans le regretter.
"Herve has an old car without regretting it."
f. Cette vielle bagnole est à Hervé (*sans le regretter).
"That old car belongs to Herve (without regretting it)."
g. Il a besoin d'un nouveau dentifrice sans le savoir.
"He needs a new tooth paste without knowing it."
h. Il lui faut un nouveau dentifrice (*sans le savoir).
"He needs a new tooth paste (without knowing it)."
i. Je connaissais le bois de Boulogne sans le regretter.
"I know the Boulogne woods without regretting it."
j. Le bois de Boulogne, ça me connaissait (*sans le regretter).
"I know the Boulogne woods (without regretting it)."
k. Hervé a bénéficié de cela sans le regretter.
"Herve benefited from that without regretting it."
l. Cela a bénéficié à Hervé (*sans le regretter).
"Herve benefited from that (without regretting it)."
m. Hervé connaît cela sans s'en rendre compte.
"Herve knows that without realizing it."
n. Cela lui est connu (*sans s'en rendre compte).
"That is known to hir (without realizing it)."

Given (197) then, the inversion hypothesis about nonstandard CIC sentences makes relevant predictions about the distribution of S-Phrases in CIC complements: S-Phrases should NOT occur in any of these associated with what the inversion hypothesis analyzes as an inversion nominal. This prediction is only testable to the extent that S-Phrases are independently allowed in CIC complements. But they are.

(203) a. Ce qui est arrivé a fait partir sans rien dire la tante de Jean.
"What happened made Jean's aunt leave without saying anything." (Kayne 1975: 216)
b. Cela fera venir Hervé sans s'en plaindre.
"That will make Herve come without complaining about it."
c. Cela le lui fera manger sans protester.
"That will make hir eat it without protesting."

One can then initially test the predicted incompatibility of nonstandard sentences and S-Phrases, as follows:[34]

(204) a. (i) Cela a fait se connaître ces gens (sans le regretter).
(ii) Cela a fait connaître ces gens l'un à l'autre (*sans le regretter).
"That made these people know each other (without regretting it)."
b. (i) Cela a fait se connaître Hervé (sans le regretter).
(ii) Cela a fait connaître Hervé à lui-même (*sans le regretter).
(iii) ?Cela a fait connaître lui-même à Hervé (*sans le regretter).
"That made Herve know himself (without regretting it)."

Those reflexive sentences that I argued earlier involve inversion complements are incompatible with S-Phrases, while essential paraphrases earlier taken to be antipassive clauses are not. But given the relevant distinct analyses, the latter satisfy (197), while the former do not.

Next, one should examine nonreflexive complements with S-Phrases. Here, since inversion is optional, there can exist noninversion structures of a sort which, even with *(re)connaître* and *voir,* are predicted to be compatible with S-Phrases. But if one chooses structures which, under a noninversion analysis, would violate FC, then their only possible analyses are inversion structures. Therefore (197) predicts that such examples should not permit an S-Phrase to be associated with the underlying complement 1. Consider then (205):

(205) a. Je vous ferai connaître à Hervé (sans le regretter).
"I will make Herve know (meet) you (without my regretting it)."
b. Cela vous fera connaître Hervé (sans le regretter).
"That will make you know (meet) Herve (without your regretting it)."
c. Cela vous fera connaître à Hervé (*sans le regretter).
"That will make Herve know (meet) you (without his regretting it)."

d. Cela les fera connaître à Hervé (sans le regretter).
"That will make Herve know (meet) them (without his regretting it)."

e. Cela les fera choisir/épouser à Hervé (sans le regretter).
"That will make Herve choose/marry them (without his regretting it)."

As predicted, (205a) is interpretable only with the S-Phrase associated with the main clause 1 represented by *je*. Association with *Hervé* is blocked, because given the existence of the fancy *vous* corresponding to the head of a 2-arc postimage, the only analysis of the complement consistent with FC is an inversion structure. But rule (197) governing S-Phrases can then not be satisfied by the complement-initial 1. Sentence (205b) is compatible with (197) because it can be analyzed as a case of noninversion, with the main clause *vous* corresponding to a 3-arc postimage of a final 1-arc in accord with rule (197).[35] Sentence (205c), with its fancy main clause 2, is only analyzable in a way consistent with FC as an inversion structure. Its initial complement 1 can then not satisfy rule (197), and the long version is predictably ungrammatical. Sentence (205d) is, however, analyzable as a noninversion structure, since FC is not relevant, and thus its long version should be as well-formed as that of (205e) based on standard Vs. For both complements can be noninversion structures without any conflict with FC. It is notable though that presumably for the same reasons which arose in the discussion of MAs, examples like (205d) are sometimes judged as ungrammatical. My guess is that this is also because of judgments based on the possibility of analyzing such an example as an inversion structure, for that analysis then fails to meet (197).

Overall then, it seems correct that as predicted by the inversion hypothesis, S-Phrases are compatible with the underlying 1s of nonstandard complements only in those cases which FC would permit to have noninversion analyses. Thus, otherwise-mysterious limitations on the distribution of S-Phrases in the CIC, like the contrast between (205c) and (205d), follow from the interaction of (197) with the inversion hypothesis.

4.4 Adverbial Expressions and 'Inherently' Reflexive Vs

Sections 4.1–4.3 worked out three distinct rules governing the distribution of various adverbial constituents. These entail at least one shared feature: in each case, ignoring certain cases with P-Phrases controlled by an initial non-1, the nominal associated with the relevant adverbial must head an arc with a 1-arc local realization. This cannot be simplified to just 'head a 1-arc', because of cases like (150b), (151a,b), (158b), (159), (167a), and (168a) involving P-Phrases at least in the looser P-Phrase dialect. These rules support the inversion hypothesis about nonstandard CIC clauses, because they predict actual contrasts between the behavior of what this hypothesis takes to be inversion 3s and that of other main clause 3s which are complement final 1s. Some rather extraordinary facts common to all the adverbial types considered support the correctness of the common feature just noted.

These involve the behavior of these adverbials in association with Vs taking 'inherent' reflexive PCs. Each of the three adverbial types can be associated with the final 1 of these in simple clauses.

(206) Hervé s'est couché/éloigné/levé/promené/tu
 a. avec enthousiasme.
 b. pour vous plaire.
 c. sans s'en rendre compte.
 "Herve lay down/went away/got up/took a walk/shut up
 a. with enthusiasm."
 b. to please you."
 c. without realizing it."

As touched on in section 3.4, some 'inherent' PCs have the option of failing to occur when such Vs appear in CIC complements. Strikingly though, this optionality is NOT independent of the three adverbial types.

(207) a. On a fait se/∅ coucher/éloigner/lever/promener/asseoir Hervé.
 "One/we made Herve lie down/go away/get up/take a walk/sit down."
 b. On a fait se/*∅ coucher/éloigner/lever/promener/asseoir Hervé
 i. avec enthousiasme.
 ii. pour vous plaire.
 iii. sans s'en rendre compte.
 "One/we made Herve lie down/go away/get up/take a walk/sit down
 i. with enthusiasm."
 ii. in order to please you."
 iii. without realizing it."

Rather amazingly, the missing reflexive PC option is incompatible with an MA, a P-Phrase, or an S-Phrase. This is especially notable, since otherwise speakers tend to prefer the form without the reflexive PC. Significantly, this apparently bizarre feature of (207bi–iii) can be taken as a simple consequence of respective principles (122), (155), and (197), if we adopt (1) the unaccusative hypothesis for the relevant Vs; (2) the view that the 'inherent' reflexive PCs are reflexes of copy arcs determined by the advancement to 1 of the unaccusative 2; and (3) a key idea of Fauconnier's (1983), already touched on several times and supported in Legendre (1986).[36] The latter view is that, in CIC complements, unaccusative (possibly all) 2-to-1 Advancement is only optional.[37]

In these terms, a missing reflexive PC CIC complement is therefore a clause in which the unaccusative 2 does NOT advance to 1, hence in which there can be no copy; see (209c) below. In that structure, the existence of the copy 2-arc E clearly depends on the advancement to 1, for only that yields the 1-arc local successor C which is one of the two sponsors of the copy-arc replacer, such replacers requiring two sponsors by definition. Therefore in a case without advancement, the original unaccusative 2 HEADS NO 1-ARC; see (209d). This predicts that such unaccusatives will systematically fail to manifest properties which are associated with the heads of 1-arcs but not with the heads of 2-arcs.

Legendre (1986) has argued that Fauconnier's idea can serve to account for the following otherwise bizarre pattern typical of 'object raising' structures in her dialect.

(208) a. Cet homme est difficile à faire *se/∅ taire.
"That man is difficult to make be quiet."
b. Le blessé sera difficile à faire *s'/∅ asseoir.
"The wounded person will be difficult to make sit down."

That is, the nominal associated with an 'inherently' reflexive unaccusative is, when part of a CIC complement, only object-raisable when the reflexive PC is absent. Legendre shows that the difference follows from a condition on the 2-arc headed by the object-raised nominal in the complement of *difficile*. In current terms, this condition is essentially that any remote predecessor of this 2-arc must also be a 2-arc.[38] Therefore in cases like (208), all the complement arcs headed by *Cet homme* and *Le blessé* must be 2-arcs. Thus the cases with *se* are bad because in these the complement 2 has advanced to 1 and the relevant nominals head 1-arcs in the complements whose predicates are *se taire* and *s'asseoir*. But in those without *se*, there is no advancement and the launchers are 2-arcs, satisfying the remote predecessor condition.

Notably, the same assumptions about failure of advancement in structures with 'inherent' reflexive Vs in which the reflexive PC is missing combine with rules (122), (155), and (197), to predict the patterns in (207bi–iii). For there is no way these rules can be satisfied by a 2 of a clause which does not advance to 1.[39]

Assumption (2) above—the view that the 'inherent' reflexive cases with missing CIC complement PCs are due to nonadvancement in the complement—can be supported further. Under this view, the final structures of the complements in pairs like (209a,b) differ radically, as in (209c,d), respectively.

(209) a. Hervé a fait se taire Louise.
b. Hervé a fait taire Louise.
"Herve made Louise be quiet."
c.

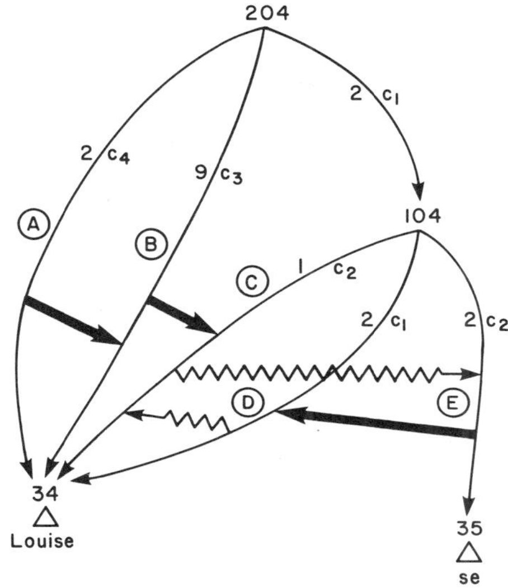

d.

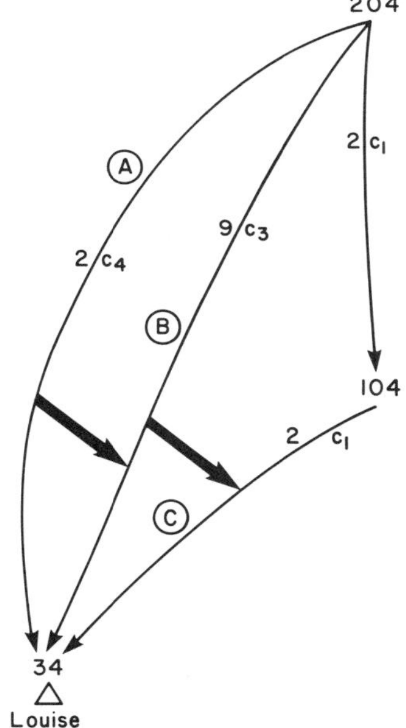

These complements thus differ, in that *Louise* heads a final 1-arc launcher in the former and a final 2-arc launcher in the latter.

While I cannot here consider any general account of coordination, it is certainly independently true of French that in a clear sense, two clauses sharing a final 1 and a final 2 CANNOT correspond to more reduced coordinations in the way that clauses sharing final 1s or sharing final 2s can. For example, compare (210) and (211) with (212):

(210) a. Hervé connaît Marie et il aime Louise.
"Herve knows Marie and he likes Louise."
b. C'est Hervé qui connaît Marie et l'aime.
"It is Herve who knows Marie and likes her."
c. C'est Hervé qui connaît Marie et aime Louise.
"It is Herve who knows Marie and likes Louise."

(211) a. Hervé connaît Marie et (il) l'aime.
"Herve knows Marie and (he) likes her."
b. Hervé connaît et (Jacques) aime Marie.
"Herve knows and (Jacques) likes Marie."
c. C'est Marie que Hervé connaît et (Jacques) aime.
"It is Marie that Herve knows and (Jacques) likes."

(212) a. Marie a insulté le directeur et il va la virer.
"Marie insulted the director and he is going to fire her."
b. *Marie a insulté le directeur et va la virer.[40]
"Marie insulted the director and going to fire her."
c. *C'est le directeur que Marie a insulté et va la virer.
"It is the director that Marie insulted and going to fire her."

Well-formed cases like (210b,c) have coordinated structures which share final 1s, while in the grammatical (211b,c) the coordinated phrases share final 2s. But *(212b,c) are bad, presumably because the shared element underlying the coordination is a final 1 of one phrase but a final 2 of the other.

If, therefore, complements like those in (209a,b) contrast, in that the former manifests a final 1 and the latter a final 2, one might well expect this contrast to manifest in the same kind of coordination blockages seen in *(212b,c). And it does:

(213) a. J'ai fait s'asseoir et se taire Marie.
b. J'ai fait asseoir et taire Marie.
c. *J'ai fait asseoir et se taire Marie.
d. *J'ai fait s'asseoir et taire Marie.
"I made Marie sit down and be quiet."

There are reduced conjunctions corresponding only to those cases which, under present assumptions, would either both involve final 1s or both involve final 2s. The mixed cases are blocked. Given Fauconnier's assumption, adopted here, one can presumably attribute this to the same principles underlying *(212b,c). But under traditional views, where the difference between (209a,b) is just one of PC presence or absence, the pattern in (213) is mysterious.

The same assumptions make predictions about other coordinations than those in (213), where 'inherent' reflexive Vs are involved. It is predicted that the (209a) type should coordinate with ordinary transitive or unergative clauses, but that the (209b) type should not. This appears to be true.

(214) a. On nous a fait nous asseoir et le manger.
b. *On nous a fait asseoir et le manger.
"One had us sit down and eat it."
c. Martin les fera s'asseoir et chanter.
d. *Martin les fera asseoir et chanter.
e. Martin les fera chanter et s'asseoir.
f. *Martin les fera chanter et asseoir.
"Martin will make them sit down and sing."

Overall then, conjunction facts seem to strongly support the possibility of nonadvancement in CIC unaccusative complements.

Fauconnier's suggestion (3) requires, as he notes (1983: 204) and as considered earlier, a limited weakening of the traditional RG/APG Final 1-Arc Law. In its APG version, the latter (Johnson and Postal 1980: 228) says that every basic clause has a final 1-arc. It could be weakened to require this, roughly, only of basic clauses at least one of whose arcs are SURFACE arcs. This would properly exclude CU complements, hence CIC complements under present assumptions, since, as stressed in chapter 2, all CU complement arcs are erased. One way to formalize this approach would be to define the notion SEMISURFACE arc as one having a neighbor which is a surface (unerased) arc. Every surface arc is then a semisurface arc, but not conversely. One could then propose to replace Johnson and Postal's (1980: 228) PN Law 44 with (215):

(215) The Weak Final 1-Arc Law
If A⟨b⟩ is a semisurface P-arc, then ⟨b⟩'s final stratum contains a 1-arc.

Since no P-arc having a U-arc foreign successor is ever a semisurface arc, CU complements satisfy (215) vacuously regardless of whether they have final 1s.

Given the viability of the relevant assumptions, facts like (207) would seem to provide further arguments for principles (122), (155), and (197), which themselves provide considerable support for the inversion hypothesis. For the otherwise-mysterious ill-formedness in *(207b) is, under current assumptions, a function of the same 1-arc-referencing limitations on various adverbial expressions which predict the incompatibility of nonstandard CIC clauses with these expressions. But the latter prediction follows only if a standard transitive analysis is rejected in favor of some analysis of the relevant CIC complements under which rules like (122), (155), and (197) cannot be satisfied by the appropriate nominals. An inversion structure is just such an analysis, and no viable alternative with this property suggests itself.

Five

FC and Counterfactual Contexts

Despite earlier claims (e.g. in chap. 1, note 9) about the absolute character of FC in the form of French studied here, certain sentences that have never to my knowledge been considered with respect to this constraint provide evidence which is relevant to its character and hence, in particular, relevant to the viability of the current formulation of FC in (56). Recall that (56) specifies that the postimage of an arc accusative at c_{final} must be plain. The latter notion was characterized only very informally, as meaning that the head of the relevant arc was third person and nonreflexive.

But, despite standard FC violations like those in (216a), in COUNTERFACTUAL conditional contexts like (216b) the relevant expressions with *à* are well-formed:

(216) a. *Hervé me fera repasser à Louise.
"Herve will have Louise iron me."
b. Si j'étais une chemise, Hervé me ferait repasser à Louise.
"If I were a shirt, Herve would have Louise iron me."

Significantly, the judgment of (216b) is made by the same speaker who sharply rejects (i) and (ii) in chapter 1, note 9. Clearly there is no way to keep (216b) compatible with a variant of FC which merely references the morphology of PCs. To this extent, such cases might suggest that something like (56), which does not reference PCs, is more adequate. But (56) itself does not seem to draw the distinction between (216a,b) and is apparently incompatible with the latter. Let us refer to the well-formedness of (216b) as the FC OVERRIDE PHENOMENON (FCOP). Various approaches to the deep problem provided by FCOP suggest themselves. Many might conclude that the facts in (216) show that the constraint involved in FC is actually 'semantic' and thus that (216a) is not really ungrammatical but somehow 'anomalous'. I will rather sketch, though quite informally, an approach to this problem which maintains the traditional view that FC is a syntactic constraint. Before I get to this, it is necessary to clarify some basic facts which delimit the scope of the phenomenon.

First, not only counterfactual conditional contexts permit FCOP. FCOP is also found, for example, in counterfactual dream contexts:

(217) J'ai rêvé que j'étais une chemise et qu'Hervé voulait me faire laver à Marie.
"I dreamed that I was a shirt and that Herve wanted to have Mary wash me."

But although conditionality seems irrelevant, counterfactuality seems crucial for FCOP, since examples like (218) are rejected when a postimage 3-arc is involved.

(218) Puisque je suis une chemise, Marie me fera laver *à/par Jacques.

The existence of cases like (216) might well suggest that a solution to FCOP is simply that FC is a restriction on the heads of certain postimages of 2-arcs when these heads reference animate objects. This could imply that such a referential condition should be built into a richer version of FC itself.

However, there is a rather strong argument against the step just envisaged. This is based on the fact that FCOP is directly paralleled by similar phenomena involving distinct French grammatical constraints. The first concerns reflexive passive (*se moyen*) constructions and was discovered by Yves-Charles Morin (pers. com. 11 May 1981). In general, French reflexive passives are difficult, but at least for many speakers by no means impossible, to construct when the passive 1 is a human nominal. For some speakers it may be necessary in this case to extract the human nominal and have the copy pronoun *cela/ça* as final 1; see Dorel 1980: 46n. 8. For others, including my principal consultant, this is not necessary. Ruwet (1972: 97) cites (220), and others accept (221) as well:

(220) Les enfants, ça se lave en dix minutes.
"The children can be washed in ten minutes."

(221) a. Les enfants se lavent en dix minutes.
"The children are washed in ten minutes."
b. Ils se lavent en dix minutes.
"They are washed in ten minutes."

Like most similar cases with human 1s, these structures are ambiguous and are interpreted either as reflexive passives or as ordinary reflexive structures, that is, with underlying 'coreferential' 1 and 2.

Despite the existence of reflexive passives with human 1s, there is a well-known (Sandfeld 1928: 133) constraint which excludes the reflexive passive analysis when the final 1 is non–third person. Hence even speakers accepting e.g. a reflexive passive reading of (221b) find all of (222) unambiguously NONPASSIVE:

(222) a. Nous nous lavons en dix minutes.
"We wash ourselves in ten minutes."
b. Vous vous lavez en dix minutes.
"You wash yourselves in ten minutes."
c. Je me lave en dix minutes.
"I wash myself in ten minutes."

So there is apparently a constraint precluding FANCY final 1s for reflexive passives.[1]

But Morin observed that in the counterfactual environment of (216b), this additional constraint referencing the non–third person property does not hold. For Morin himself, his informants, and my own consultant, the examples of (223) are entirely correct on reflexive passive readings for the second clause.

(223) a. Si tu étais une chemise, tu te vendrais mal.
"If you were a shirt, you would sell badly."
b. Si nous étions de chemises, nous nous vendrions pour pas cher.
"If we were shirts, we would sell pretty cheaply."

The parallelism between this phenomenon—call it the REFLEXIVE PASSIVE PERSON OVERRIDE (RPPO)—and FCOP is shown further by the fact that RPPO is also found in dream contexts.

(224) J'ai rêvé que j'étais une (mauvaise) chemise, et que je me vendais mal.
"I dreamed that I was a (bad) shirt, and that I was selling badly."

So sentence (224) is interpretable with the last clause as a reflexive passive.[2]

Moreover, a third grammatical principle appears to be overridden in the same environments. A well-known French rule is that in the presence of a (accusative or dative) REFLEXIVE PC, the past tense auxiliary must be *être* and not *avoir,* even with Vs which otherwise require the latter:

(225) a. Marcel l'a/*l'est décrit.
"Marcel described him."
b. Marcel *s'a/s'est décrit.
"Marcel described himself."

(226) a. Lucienne et Georges les ont/*les sont contactés.
"Lucienne and Georges contacted them."
b. Lucienne et Georges *s'ont/se sont contactés.
"Lucienne and Georges contacted each other."

But there are contexts where this constraint appears to be overridden. Burston (1979: 154n) cites example (227) from an article by H. Sten:

(227) A sa place, jura Michaud, je ne m'aurais pas foutu dehors en me traitant de cinglé.
"In her position, swore Michaud, I would not have thrown me out while calling me crazy."

The superficial 1 in (227) is *je,* and there is an accusative PC *me;* nonetheless the auxiliary is a form of *avoir.* Moreover, as Burston stresses: "Given the situation described, wherein the subject literally is seen to act upon itself as if it were another entity, it is the only grammatical possibility." He is saying that the choice of the other auxiliary would yield a sentence with a different meaning. The same point holds for the English translation, which reveals apparent override, under the same conditions, of the constraint requiring a reflexive form. But substitution of *myself* for the first *me* in the translation of (227) yields a different meaning, in fact exactly that of the relevant French case with the normal reflexive auxiliary *être*. These properties are unchanged if one replaces a counterfactual phrase like *à sa place* by a more explicit *Si j'avais été à sa place* 'If I had been in his place', or *Si j'avais été lui* 'If I had been him'.

Since FC, the reflexive passive constraint, and the auxiliary constraint, as well as the reflexive condition in English, are all overridden in the same counterfactual environments, it would clearly be a mistake to build this fact into separate ad hoc conditions on these rules. Rather, there should be general principles, valid for French constructions and—on the basis of the similarity with English—possibly for NLs in general, which predict the behavior in counterfactual contexts of certain forms which syntactically LOOK as if they were non–third person or reflexive but which behave as if they were not. In short, some principles should in certain contexts somehow permit the syntactic nature of certain forms to be partly different from what their morphological shapes suggest. These principles would somehow determine that nominals having the superficial syntax of non–third person nominals nonetheless behave like third person nominals when occurring in the relevant contexts.

I have no proposal about how to actually formulate the required conditions. But informally, certain ideas seem plausible. Their logic involves an analysis which takes account of the claim, which I consider correct, that an example like e.g. (216b) is a paraphrase of (228):

(228) Si j'étais une chemise, Hervé ferait repasser cette chemise-là/celle-là à Louise.
"If I were a shirt, Herve would have Louise iron that shirt/that one."

In other words, the second clause in these sentences talks about the ironing—in a world distinct from the presumed real world—of a shirt, not about the ironing of a person. If so, the subordinate clause of a sentence like (216b) contains a nominal which has the semantic properties of the predicate nominal of the counterfactual clause but which matches grammatically the 1 of that clause. The same point is shown by English analogues. For instance, (229a) seems equivalent to (229b):

(229) a. If you were an integer, we could factor you into primes.
b. If you were an integer, we could factor that integer into primes.

Thus, while the nominal *you* in the first clause of (229a) designates a person, the *you* in its second clause clearly designates an integer. That is, the 2s of the V *factor* have the same denotations in both (229a,b).

If this view is correct, then one natural approach to the phenomena under discussion would involve a special kind of anaphora limited—perhaps by grammatical law, but minimally, in a way valid for French and English—to counterfactual contexts, permitting an anaphoric element which is actually linked to a predicational element (e.g. *an integer* in (229a)) to have a form appropriate for an anaphoric element linked to the 1 of that predicational element. Thus the basic facts would reduce to principles which permit an anaphor A linked to certain predicational elements to have a morphological structure otherwise appropriate for an anaphor linked to the 1 of these predicational elements. In these terms, in examples like (229a), the underlying 2 of the V *factor* is not a second person nominal but a third person nominal, and analogous claims hold for all of the three types of French case.

Thus, in (216b), under these assumptions, the postimage of the 2-arc launcher would be pronominal element linked to *une chemise,* hence third person, consistent with FC as represented in (56). In (224), the underlying 2 of the reflexive passive clause would also be an anaphoric element linked to *une chemise,* permitting an account of the reflexive passive person constraint requiring that the 2-arc local predecessor of the 1-arc local successor defining the clause as a passive have a third person head. Finally, in (227), the 1 of the clause whose auxiliary is unexpectedly a form of *avoir* would be an anaphoric element linked to *sa,* hence not linked to the first person 2 of the clause. Thus there is no reflexive connection internal to that clause, and the potential exists for explaining the presence of the nonreflexive auxiliary. So, as desired, the informal proposal I have made seems to offer a single general approach to the apparent overrides of all of the constraints, both the three in French and the English constraint revealed in the gloss of (227). For again, under the assumptions at issue, there would be no reflexive relation internal to the clause 'I would not have thrown me out . . .'.

Of course it is one thing to specify the proposal just made vaguely and entirely informally and another to develop it formally internal to a specific (e.g. the APG) framework. Considerable difficult technical work is needed. In particular, an account is required of the way the morphology of anaphoric elements is determined by their real antecedents and, in the cases at hand, by nonantecedents related to those antecedents in fixed ways. So far then, the suggestion is just a promissory note. But it has, I think, enough plausibility to indicate that the override phenomenon with respect to FC, although interesting and perplexing, does not currently have great bearing on the central issue of this study, namely, the validity of the inversion hypothesis. For while FCOP raises real problems for the formulation of FC in (56), it seems, given the parallelism with RPPO, and the other constraints which are also apparently overridden, that these problems do not indicate any flaw in the formulation of (56). Rather, one can reasonably hope that these facts are effects of an unusual type of anaphora apparently allowed under the scope of counterfactual specifications. This type of anaphora seems to assign to an element anaphoric to some predicational form a morphological structure appropriate for an anaphor linked to the 1 of that predicational form.[3]

Six

Conclusions

This study has involved the working out of the interactions between (1) an abstract theoretical state of affairs and (2) an array of apparently exceptional properties of French CIC sentences based on nonstandard Vs. The starting point for (2) was the traditional observation that nonstandard sentences seemingly fail to obey the constraint called here 'FC' (= (56)). The abstract point (1) is that the analysis of the CIC sketched in section 2.2 has the consequence that the postimage pattern for an embedded CIC inversion clause, either personal or absolute, is the same for corresponding complement nominals as the pattern for an embedded transitive clause. This theoretical situation renders POSSIBLE, as first noted in effect in Frantz (1977), an analysis of 'classical' transitive CU structures as inversion structures. By 'classical' I mean those in which the apparent complement-final 1 appears as a main-clause 3, and the apparent complement-final 2 as a main-clause 2. Since the CIC has been taken as a CU structure, (1) permits a treatment of (some or all) CIC cases as involving complement inversion.[1] Thus the inversion hypothesis is the link between (1) and (2). It is a set of assumptions which combine with (1) to provide an account of (2) under which the relevant facts are not really exceptional at all. Chapters 3, 4, and 5 developed arguments supporting an inversion analysis for nonstandard complements. It was shown that an inversion analysis eliminates a variety of anomalies in the description of nonstandard structures.

It seems then that the inversion hypothesis has a considerable degree of descriptive success. In particular, it can, without much danger of exaggeration, be claimed that it provides the CURRENTLY most adequate solution of the descriptive problem involving FC, that is, of the fact that (10a,b,c,d), repeated here, are grammatical in spite of the standard situation revealed in (7), also repeated.

(10) a. On vous fera connaître à Louise.
"One/we will have Louise know (meet) you."
b. Le président s'est fait reconnaître à Louise.
"The president$_i$ had Louise recognize himself$_i$."
c. Jacques nous a fait voir à ses chefs.
"Jacques had his bosses see us."
d. André doit se faire connaître à l'agent de liaison.
"Andre must make himself known to the liaison agent."

(7) a. *Marcel vous a fait épouser au medecin.
"Marcel had the doctor marry you."
b. *On nous a fait choisir à Jacques.
"One had Jacques choose us."
c. *Cette vedette se fera oublier à ton collègue.
"That (film) star will make your colleague forget her."

The security of the judgment of superiority for the inversion hypothesis stands on the fact that, to my knowledge, there is almost no extant competing account of (10).[2] Previous work, e.g. Kayne (1975: 298 n), seems not to have gone beyond noting such examples as exceptional. Notably, as a solution to the apparent exceptions to FC, the inversion hypothesis also serves as the basis for a solution to a number of other otherwise exceptional features of nonstandard sentences. This correlation supports the view that the assumptions underlying the inversion hypothesis are not ad hoc devices designed to save an artificially exceptionless formulation of FC from cases like (10).

The basic logic appealed to was essentially this. Nonstandard Vs show a number of apparently special and irregular properties. These can, given the theoretical framework adopted, specifically (1), essentially be reduced to a single unpredictable fact, associated with a major subcondition. The fact is that these Vs are ALLOWED to appear in inversion clauses, that is, in clauses which contain 3-arc local successors of 1-arcs, but ONLY IF these are CIC complements. The subcondition is that nonstandard Vs occur only with CIC main V *faire*.

Some linguists may regard it as peculiar, methodologically impermissible, or intractably complex to limit the occurrence of specific Vs in inversion clauses just to CIC complements and with a specific main V.[3] But in APG terms, neither type of restriction is particularly troubling or difficult, given the specific account of CU structures sketched in chapter 2. For recall that the key property of a CU construction is that a complement P-arc has a U-arc foreign successor in the immediately dominating main clause; that U-arc is hence a neighbor of the main clause P-arc. Therefore, all the restrictions just referred to reduce to constraints linking elements in the substructure in (231).

(231) The Restricted Inversion Environments

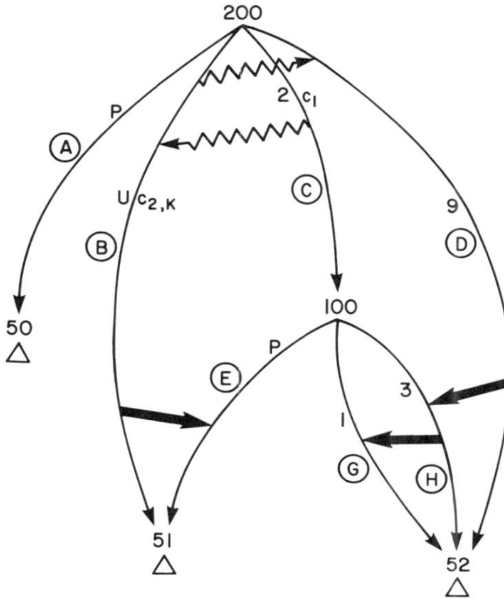

That is, the constraints limit the existence of 3-arc local successors like H with a particular predicate node like 51 to just the case where 51 heads a U-arc neighbor of a P-arc like A whose head has the V *faire* as head of its Stem branch.

The posited constraints on CIC inversion are just further subconditions to be added to the general condition French needs anyway to limit the possibilities of inversion. One can assume that there is a overall rule to this effect, limiting inversion to certain Vs, as informally specified in (232):

(232) General Constraint on French Inversion (First Version)
If A⟨b⟩ is a 3-arc local successor of a 1-arc and B⟨b⟩ is a P-arc, then B's V-stem is a member of the set {X}.

Most French Vs will obviously NOT be listed in the set referenced in (232) and thus cannot be the predicates of inversion clauses UNDER ANY CIRCUMSTANCES. Vs so excluded include standard CIC complement Vs like those heading the complement clauses in (7).

Although nonstandard Vs WILL be listed in (232), the class of inversion clauses permitted by this is further pared down by a condition linking nonstandard inversion to CIC complements and to a particular main V. Let us informally introduce the term CRANE to designate a relation between the P-arc of a CU main clause and any launcher in the complement of that clause. Given this, the restrictions in question can be sketched as in (233):

(233) Constraint on French Nonstandard Inversion
If A⟨b⟩ is a 3-arc local successor of a 1-arc, and B⟨b⟩ is a P-arc whose V-stem is a member of {NONSTANDARD}, then A is a prelauncher and the V-stem of A's crane is *faire*.

Here NONSTANDARD is the name of the set containing the three Vs we have seen allow inversion essentially only in CIC complements, and also any others which might be discovered which behave in the same way. The constraints at issue are thus neither hard to state precisely nor unnatural in any obvious sense, since they involve relations between elements closely connected in definite ways in the relevant PNs, as shown in (231).[4] Note that in (231) A is H's crane.

Moreover, given their logical structure, (232) and (233) can be combined into a single overall rule specifying the conditions on lexically governed French inversion:

(234) General Constraint on French Inversion (Final Version)
If A⟨b⟩ is a 3-arc local successor of a 1-arc and V_x is the V-stem of a P-arc B⟨b⟩, then V_x is a member of {X}; and if V_x is a member of {NONSTANDARD}, then A is a prelauncher and the V-stem of A's crane is *faire*.

In present terms, (234) is in effect the account of most of the various idiosyncrasies of clauses based on nonstandard Vs—their (only) apparent failure to obey constraints like FC, RFX1, etc. Under the inversion hypothesis, these uneliminable irregularities thus reduce to the question of which Vs can idiosyncratically appear in inversion structures limited to CIC complements. The reason why e.g. *connaître* CIC complements APPEAR to violate FC but *critiquer* complements don't is simply that (234) allows the former to occur in CIC inversion complements, but not the latter. But it is independently supportable, especially via the arguments in Harris (1981), that an adequate theory of NLs has to allow for idiosyncratic constraints on the appearance of Vs in inversion structures. However, there is no known reason to believe that a constraint like FC need be sensitive to lexical citations. Hence another minor basis for adopting the inversion hypothesis is that it reduces an array of French anomalies to the sort of irregularity which grammatical theory arguably needs to recognize in any event.

A methodological argument similar to that just given involves RFX1. As shown in chapter 3, under the inversion hypothesis RFX1 can be stated simply and with no exceptions (if informally) as in (30). But under other views, the existence of examples like (12b), repeated here, requires a more complex formulation.

(12) b. La psychiatrie a fait connaître Marcel à lui-même.
"Psychiatry made Marcel know himself."

However, as was noted, the only factual basis for a formulation more complex than (30) is the class of CIC sentences based on *connaître*. So the inversion hypothesis avoids an extremely undesirable consequence. This is the necessity of formulating a basic pronominalization constraint in complicated terms, where the complications are motivated internal to French only by the facts in multiclause sentences involving a single embedded V. Under the inversion hypothesis, the apparent violations of RFX1 reduce again to the membership of the class {NONSTANDARD} in rule (234). This argument would become absolutely overwhelming if, as speculated in chapter 1, note 6, RFX1 were a grammatical law. For it is impossible for a law to be suspended under any circumstances, and thus a fortiori in the case of a single French V. The basic conclusion is that the inversion hypothesis reduces irregularities with respect to a diverse body of constraints essentially to a question of which Vs can occur in inversion clauses, a matter grammatical theory must deal with independently of the CIC or of French in general.

At the beginning of this study, it was claimed that the fact that the number of nonstandard Vs was small was of no significance. One reason is that the logic of the arguments just given is independent of the number of Vs which have to be specified as subject to special conditions on their appearance in inversion clauses. But another far more basic reason is that the truth of claims about sentence structures involving one V is in no way dependent on there being other Vs subject to the same or similar claims. It is thus irrelevant to claims about English *be* that there is no other English V with the same auxiliary properties, and it is irrelevant to claims about *wish* that there is no other English V permitting the same kind of 'subjunctive' complements:

(235) I wish/*hope/*want/*believe/*expect/*grant/*doubt that I were young.

Assume now that the general argument of this study is correct, and that while standard sentences have finally transitive complements, nonstandard sentences DO have inversion complements. What is the significance of this conclusion beyond its implications for French grammar? There seem to be three principal sorts of answer. First, INTERNAL to relational frameworks, the results of this work support various relational ideas, including those in (236a–d), and disconfirm that in (236e).

(236) a. Inversion clauses exist.

b. As first suggested by Fauconnier (1983), the Final 1-Arc Law does NOT require a final 1-arc in CU complements, a claim embodied in the replacement of the original version of that principle by the Weak Final 1-Arc Law in (215).

c. Hence, a clause not required by the latter law to have a final 1-arc can be an absolute inversion clause. And absolute inversion clauses do exist.

d. An otherwise apparently viable set of universal constraints on postimages are such that the apparent 3-arc postimage of a 1-arc can turn out to be the 3-arc postimage of an (inversion) 3-arc.
e. Contra the hypothesis of Frantz (1977), not all CU complements are INTRANSITIVE, since French STANDARD CU complements are not.[5]

EXTERNAL to relational frameworks, however, the chief importance of the conclusions of this study probably involves the question of the existence of 'abstract' grammatical structure, that is, grammatical structure which cannot be interpreted as an aspect of surface representations. At one time it seemed that this question had been unequivocally resolved in favor of the existence of a rich domain of abstract grammatical form. This apparent resolution was coextensive with the apparent justification for the ideas of transformational grammar. In recent years, however, it has become widely accepted that the motivations for transformational grammar were by no means as definitive as they had appeared or as had been claimed. And a large body of work, including Bach (1981), Brame (1978, 1979, 1980, 1981), Dowty (1978, 1979, 1982a, 1982b), Cooper (1983), Gazdar (1981a, 1981b, 1982), Gazdar, Pullum, and Sag (1982), Gazdar, Klein, Pullum, and Sag (1985), and Sag (1982, 1983), has, in effect, called into question the existence of abstract grammatical structure. The results of the present study are, I believe, some among many conclusions internal to relational work which support abstract structure, though of course of a kind different from that assumed in transformational work. If sustainable, these results thereby falsify the view that the grammatical structure of an arbitrary NL sentence can always be identified with the surface structure of that sentence. Indeed, if the present conclusions stand, the kind of inversion uncovered here provides an example of an especially troubling type (for those rejecting abstract structure) of the sort of thing which could not exist were the antiabstract position correct.

Recall that it turns out that the properties of sentences like (237a,b) can be regularized by assuming that their complements are inversion structures:

(237) a. Marcel nous a fait voir à Louise.
"Marcel had Louise see us."
b. Cela nous a fait connaître à nous-mêmes.
"That made us know ourselves."

While this view integrates directly and naturally with the abstract clause union view of CIC sentences based on the framework in chapter 2, it has no interpretation at all in purely surface terms. From the latter point of view, (237a) should have the same general surface structure as (238a,b):

(238) a. *Marcel nous a fait regarder à Louise.
"Marcel had Louise look at us."
b. *Cela nous a fait comprendre à nous-mêmes.
"That made us understand ourselves."

But the latter structures are ungrammatical. The point is not, of course, that surface approaches cannot distinguish (237) from *(238) in some way. Via the recognition of special grammatical categories or features, any structures can always be distinguished. But what seems beyond the scope of such approaches is any means of analyzing (237) in such a way that each of the principles which block *(238a,b) and other similar cases can be stated in as general a form as if (237), etc., did not exist. And this seems to follow from the very nature of the surface assumption, which simply has no place for a locus of structure where it would make sense to say that the complements of (237) involve inversion while those of *(238) do not.

It is important, I think, that the rejection of abstract structure contemplated internal to the new trend referred to just above has in general been justified only vis-à-vis transformational ideas. There have been few attempts by proponents of purely surface approaches to deal with the kinds of abstract structure putatively justified by relational work, of which the present investigation is but one small example.

Beyond questions of abstract structure, the present conclusions also bear on the adequacy of nonrelational frameworks which do recognize types of abstract structure, e.g. variants of transformational grammar. Certain aspects of relational analyses can, in part, certainly be simulated in transformational terms. For example, many, but by no means all, successor relations can be simulated by e.g. movement rules. Moreover, even when it seems that a particular successor structure could be modeled by transformational derivation, it can turn out that those successor analyses are clearly incompatible with certain versions of transformational theories. Specifically, inversion structures turn out to be incompatible with a movement simulation in the government-binding (GB) framework of Chomsky (1981, 1982) and many derivative publications.[6] There are two relevant subcases, absolute inversion structures and personal ones. Consider the former first.

Simulation of absolute inversion via NP movement is outright incompatible with the GB framework. The problem is that inversion would have to be simulated by movement of an NP from subject position to a position in a verb phrase, possibly to a position inside a prepositional phrase inside that verb phrase. But in the GB framework, a moved phrase is linked to a trace, and this linkage must meet various 'binding' conditions. But these are clearly violated in a structure like e.g. (239c), taken as a movement simulation from a base structure like (239b) of an inversion analysis for (239a), argued in section 3.4 to have an absolute inversion complement.

(239) a. Cela a fait connaître lui-même à Marcel.
"That made Marcel know himself."
b. . . . ⟨ ⟨Marcel⟩ ⟨connaître lui-même ⟨ ⟨à⟩ ⟨e_j⟩⟩⟩⟩
c. . . . ⟨$_S$ ⟨$_{NP}e_i$⟩ ⟨$_{VP}$connaître lui-même ⟨$_{PP}$⟨$_P$à⟩ ⟨$_{NP}$Marcel$_i$⟩⟩⟩⟩

One problem is that the trace e_i is clearly not properly bound by the moved nominal *Marcel*$_i$. The structure is thus not licit internal to the GB framework even IF, as represented in (239), the moved element has shifted to a nonargument position, that is, one previously occupied by an empty node, as required of all movements in this framework.

Moreover, structure (239c) is illegal for different reasons. It is claimed (see Chomsky 1981: 37) that every position strictly subcategorized by a lexical head is 'theta-marked' (assigned a thematic role) by that head. Further, it is assumed that the position of a prepositional phrase object is a strictly subcategorized one. Hence, such a position cannot be filled by a nonargument, as in (239), and movement into a *to* phrase is just as impossible as movement into a passive *by* phrase, explicitly noted to be banned in Chomsky (1982: 16).

Next consider an attempt to simulate a personal inversion structure internal to GB assumptions. This is impossible for a variety of reasons, including those just cited in connection with movement to strictly subcategorized positions. These have already led in this framework to the abandonment, mentioned in chapter 4, note 1, of the traditional transformational view that the passive *by* phrase and its analogues in other NLs are moved subjects. Consider (240b,c) as a proposed GB derivation simulating a personal inversion analysis for (240a).

(240) a. That matters to me.
b. I_j ⟨matter $that_k$ to e_l⟩
c. $That_k$ ⟨matters e_k to I_j⟩

Although the trace of *that*$_k$, e_k, is properly bound by *that*$_k$, the structure is illegal, first, because the latter phrase has moved into an argument position, that formerly occupied by I_j. And movement in GB terms is only possible to nonargument positions like that of the empty nominal e_l in the initial prepositional phrase. But second, the presence of an empty NP as prepositional object as in (239b) is not permitted, for reasons considered in discussing absolute inversion, namely, strictly subcategorized positions require assignment of a thematic role.

There is thus apparently no way in GB terms to model personal inversion (as NP movement), just as there is no way to model the relational analysis of the passive 8 as an earlier 1. The incompatibility of the GB framework with a movement account of inversion is noted by Anderson (1984: 183–84), who specifies: "Within the Government/Binding theory, inversion structures like (21) below would violate otherwise valid binding conditions if they involved genuine syntactic movement, since movement from subject to indirect object position would leave a subject trace bound only by an NP in indirect object position. Such a trace would not be c-commanded by its antecedent, and thus the structure would not be well-formed." Since the present study, like many other relational works, supports the existence of personal inversion structures, and in addition supports the existence of absolute inversion clauses, the GB assumptions precluding simulation of inversion analyses appear untenable.[7]

Notes

Introduction

1. This terminology, based on a remark of Gaatone (1976a: 165), who speaks of 'le haut degré de cohésion', is introduced and utilized in Postal (1981, 1983a, 1984). The literature on the CIC is quite extensive. Traditionally oriented studies with considerable information and varied further references include Martinon (1927), Sandfeld (1965), Grevisse (1969: 1063–66), Harmer (1979), and Danell (1979). Modern studies include Kayne (1975), Gaatone (1976a, 1976b), Seuren (1972), Cannings and Moody (1978), McA'Nulty (1978), Y.-C. Morin (1977), J.-Y. Morin (1978), Herschensohn (1981), Roberts (1980), Rouveret and Vergnaud (1980), Taraldsen (1981), Fauconnier (1983), and Tasmowski-de Ryck (1983, 1985).

2. More generally, I systematically utilize the now standard RG/APG notations for the traditionally recognized grammatical relations in (i)–(iii):

(i) Subject = 1
(ii) Direct Object = 2
(iii) Indirect Object = 3

3. For many speakers, there is a class of 'active' intransitives which permit, as an option, the complement 1 to appear as a main clause 3 in the CIC. These speakers accept sentences such as (i), (ii):

(i) On lui a fait voter pour elle.
"One/we had him/her vote for her."
(ii) Le capitaine leur a laissé tirer sur les terroristes.
"The captain let them fire on the terrorists."

Similarly, some speakers permit, with roughly the same class of embedded Vs, the complement 1 to appear in a main clause *par* phrase:

(iii) On a fait voter pour elle par les syndicalistes.
"One/we had the union members vote for her."
(iv) Le capitaine a laissé tirer sur les terroristes par ses hommes.
"The captain let the terrorists be fired on by his men."

These possibilities, which have no direct bearing on the topic of the present study, are discussed in Postal (1981, 1983a, 1984, to appear b).

4. The variants in question are the contracted forms of *à* plus the forms of the definite article:

(i) à + le = au
(ii) à + les = aux

5. In the CIC examples (2a,b,c), the complement 2 is an animate (moreover, human) nominal. It is in fact very difficult to construct well-formed CIC cases like (2) under this condition. Most such examples appear to be ill-formed, and the relevant meanings are typically expressed by sentences having the CIC pattern of (8), later taken to involve complement passives. Hence examples like (i) are more typical than (2).

(i) a. *Le gardien a fait porter Marie à Jacques.
"The watchman made Jacques carry Marie."
b. Le gardien a fait porter Marie par Jacques.
"The watchman had Marie carried by Jacques."

The constraint in *(ia) is sometimes claimed to be completely general whenever the complement 2 designates a person, for example, by Le Bidois and Le Bidois (1968: 315), as noted in Harmer (1979: 208). However, as the latter (1979: 209) remarks, and as indicated in (2), this is not truly the case. Kayne (1975: 241) and Gaatone (1976b: 529) also in effect observe the failure of the restriction in question to cover ALL transitive Vs.

6. Following Postal (1981, 1983a, 1984) I use 'hir' to gloss French third person pronominal forms which are unmarked for gender. This neologism thus serves to avoid disjunctions such as 'his or hers', 'him or her', etc.

7. The pronominal forms *lui, eux,* etc., in (5a,b,c) are traditionally called 'strong' or 'disjunctive' forms, while the PCs in (5d,e,f) are traditionally called 'weak' or 'conjunctive' forms. I prefer the term 'PC' for the latter and refer to the former as 'disjunctive'.

8. A common view (see Quicoli 1980: 148; Rouveret and Vergnaud 1980: 134; Roberts 1980: 137, 210; and Taraldsen 1981: 260) is that the CIC does not permit nonreflexive accusative (or) dative PCs corresponding to complement 2s or 3s to appear on the EMBEDDED V. For many speakers, at least, this is just not the case, although such occurrences are tightly constrained, in particular, by the requirement that the complement 1 then be represented by a main clause (dative or accusative) PC. Hence there are sentences like (i) from Bordelois (1980: 155), who remarks that they are ". . . acceptable in most dialects."

(i) Marie lui a fait le lui donner.
"Marie had hir gir it to hir."

The grammaticality of such sentences is also recognized in Morin (1977), Kayne (1975: 295n), Tasmowski-de Ryck (1983: 125), and Fauconnier (1983: 228 n. 3). Morin (1977: 19) cites:

(ii) Il lui a fait le voir.
"He had hir see it/him."

Milner (1982: 353), while rejecting (iii), accepts (iv):

(iii) *Je lui ferai lui donner une pomme.
(iv) Je la ferai lui parler.

9. Recognition of this in the literature is common, if rather unsystematic; see Sandfeld (1965: 182), Kayne (1975: 241–42, 298 n), Hyman and Zimmer (1976: 202–4), Hendrick (1978: 240–42), Danell (1979: 61 n), Rouveret and Vergnaud (1980: 143 n), Tasmowski-de Ryck (1984: 414). Some apparent disagreement is found in Cannings and Moody (1978: 342), where it is claimed: " . . . although this restriction is not absolute, as has sometimes been claimed . . . ." These authors then cite a number of putatively well-formed examples, including (i):

(i) Elle s'est fait assassiner aux/par les CRS
"She got murdered by members of the Corps Républicain de Sécurité."

But my consultant sharply rejects the version of (i) with *aux* and only accepts that with *par,* and most of the rest of the literature agrees. Similarly, Hyman and Zimmer (1976: 203) claims that two of their informants tried to imagine plausible situations where (ii) could be used:

(ii) Ils m'ont fait élever à ma pauvre grand-mère.
"They had my poor grandmother raise me."

My informant also clearly rejects this (in favor of an analogue with *par*). And Hyman and Zimmer (1976: 210) themselves strongly downgrade the importance of the supposed acceptance of (ii), noting that " . . . most of the French speakers we interrogated would not accept sentences such as . . . under any circumstances." The latter ellipsis points contained (ii). It is thus unclear to me to what extent it would be reasonable to interpret the remarks of Cannings and Moody and of Hyman and Zimmer as suggesting the existence of certain dialect differences. In any event, the present study is based on the judgments of speakers who totally reject the non-*par* variants of cases like (i) and (ii) and their parallels when the reflexive PC is replaced by a non–third person PC. But see chapter 5.

10. The fact that some PCs, e.g. *y* and *en,* alternate with prepositional phrases rather than with bare nominals, although of considerable importance in frameworks like that of Kayne (1975: chapter 2), has no real significance in the terms underlying the following discussion.

11. The assumption of a correspondence between PCs and nominals is nontrivial for reasons beyond those in the previous note, in view of such alternations as those in (i):

(i) Hervé l'est sans doute, intelligent.
"Herve is without doubt intelligent."

(ii) Qu'Hervé est intelligent, tout le monde le croit.
"That Herve is intelligent, everyone believes (it)."

In these, the PCs *l'* and *le* appear to correspond to the sorts of phrases whose status as nominals is eminently controversial. This is marginal to current interests and will not be discussed; see Postal (1985, to appear b).

12. Kayne (1975: 241) appears to suggest that the constraint in (7) is in some sense a strengthened version of that mentioned in note 5. I take no position on this matter. Note, though, that the two constraints do not systematically hold for the same Vs, as shown by the ill-formedness of (7) and the well-formedness of (2).

13. Sentence (8e) has a different structure from that which is relevant; on the latter, it means, irrelevantly, "One had us choose."

Chapter One

1. Although Kayne (1975: 372) cites a sentence nearly identical to (12b) with a question mark.

2. More precisely in APG terms, no complement 2-arc has a SUCCESSOR in the main clause; see chapter 2.

The principles which determine that the complement 1 of a clause with an accusative reflexive PC ends up as a main clause 2 are far from obvious. My view is that the conditions of section 2.2 largely suffice to determine this under an Antipassive analysis of such clauses touched on below.

Kayne (1975: 416n) cites (i), which corresponds to the simple clause (ii):

(i) La jalousie professionnelle faisait se détester les professeurs l'un l'autre.
"Professional jealousy made the professors detest each other."

(ii) Les professeurs se détestaient l'un l'autre.
"The professors detested each other."

It might appear that *l'un l'autre* is a superficial 2 of the clause in (ii) and a superficial 2 of the main clause in (i). But under the antipassive analysis just mentioned, which is associated with the accusative reflexive PC, it can be argued that although this form is a 2 at one level, it is not a superficial 2 in (ii) nor a main clause 2 at any level in (i). If to the contrary it were, the main clause would have two superficial 2s, since *les professeurs* is clearly a superficial 2. This would inter alia violate the RG Stratal Uniqueness Law; see Perlmutter and Postal (1983). The latter allows at most a single Term (1,2,3) arc per stratum.

3. One might try to reduce the facts in (20) to FC by stating the latter as a constraint on PCs rather than on nominals. Since (20b) contains no PC, it would thus not be blocked by FC. But this still leaves it obscure why the same considerations do not rescue *(20a). See chapter 5 for further discussion of FC.

4. In this case there is no parallelism with reciprocals, since reciprocal sentences on the pattern of (19b) are not possible.

(i) *J'ai décrit l'un l'autre à ces aveugles.
"I described those blind persons to each other."

The restriction blocking *(i) should then also block the reciprocal analogue of (20b) regardless of any other factors. And it does:

(ii) *La psychiatrie a fait connaître l'un l'autre à ces aveugles.
"Psychiatry made those blind persons know each other."

5. The unclear notion 'superficial' 1/2/3 turns out to correspond to the precise concept Final 1/2/3 discussed in section 2.1.

6. The constraint needs to reference the superficial status of the reflexive/reciprocal form, since passives corresponding to banned structures like (i) are reasonably acceptable in several variants as long as the superficial 1 of the passive is not a reflexive/reciprocal form:

(i) a. *Elle-même$_i$ a décrit Hervé à Joanne$_i$.
"Herself described Herve to Joanne."
b. Hervé a été décrit par Joanne$_i$ à elle-même$_i$.
"Herve was described by Joanne to herself."
c. Hervè a été décrit à Joanne$_i$ par elle-même$_i$.
"Herve was described to Joanne by herself."

But in relational terms, *elle-même* in (ic) heads an earlier (though not final) 1-arc.

Note further that disjunctive reflexive forms like that in (ia) can occur as superficial 1s; it is just anaphoric linkages which are blocked. So (ia) is well-formed on a reading where *elle-même* is not anaphorically connected to *Joanne*.

While for the purposes of this study I consider RFX1 a French rule, it may actually be a grammatical law. This would not be compatible with certain views in the literature, particularly involving antecedence of reflexives in Philippine languages. Thus, Bell (1974, 1976) argued that a reflexive in Cebuano can be a final advanced 1 of a clause, one anteceded by the earlier 1/final 8 (chômeur). Such an analysis is clearly incompatible with taking RFX1 as a law. But recent work by Donna Gerdts of the State University of New York at Buffalo suggests independently that the nominal taken by Bell to be a final 1 is not, and that the nominal taken by her to be a final 8 is actually a final (ergative) 1. If so, then Cebuano ceases to offer counterexamples to a universal interpretation of RFX1. Further, if Gerdts's analysis of Philippine clause structures is correct, the unique treatment of Tagalog 'equi' constructions in Johnson and Postal (1980), under which the invisible complement nominal is an initial but not final 1, also is eliminable in favor of a treatment of Tagalog 'equi' exactly like that of English. I conclude that taking RFX1 as one of the grammatical laws lending content to the primitive notion '1' deserves serious consideration.

However, a seemingly strong impediment to an interpretation of RFX1 as a law is found in Hubbard's (1982) account of Albanian. According to Hubbard, while in general Albanian reflexive 1s are, as predicted by RFX1 as a law, ill-formed, this is not the case for certain passive clauses, namely, when the passive 1 corresponds to an earlier 2 controlled by a 3. Thus, according to Hubbard, both (i) and (ii) are grammatical:

(i)

Artisti i a tregoi veten Dritës.
artist-the-NOM Clitic Clitic show self-ACC Drita-DAT
"The artist showed herself$_i$ to Drita$_i$."

(ii)

Vetja i u tregua Dritës prej artistit
self-NOM Clitic Clitic show Drita-DAT by artist
"Herself$_i$ was shown to Drita$_i$ by the artist."

Accepting that (ii) is grammatical on the indicated reading, saving a grammatical law interpretation of RFX1 would require showing that *Vetja* in (ii) is not a final 1. This would not appear to be an easy task.

7. Sentences like (25) are discussed in Kayne (1975: 372), which points out their relations to simple clauses. In the transformational terms Kayne adopted, he remarked:

Furthermore, FI changes the relative order of a pronoun and a coreferential NP in

(90) a. ?Cela fera connaître Jean à lui-même.
b. Je ferai connaître ces garçons l'un à l'autre.

The derivation of the latter example is

Je ferai S⟨NP⟨PRO$_i$⟩ connaître ces garçons$_i$⟩ →
Je ferai connaître ces garçons$_i$ à NP⟨PRO$_i$⟩ . . .

But Kayne seems not to have recognized the anomalous character of the anaphoric connections posited in his underlying forms, revealed by the patterns of (27)–(29).

Chapter Two

1. To many contemporary linguists, a particularly striking feature of PNs like (34) may be their failure to assign any equivalent of a VP structure to the relevant sentence. While recognition of VPs is not incompatible with the basic structural ideas of APG (or RG), it would require many unhappy complications. In particular, it would make it impossible to use the Local/Foreign distinction in the way it is currently exploited. For example, given VPs, the 1-arc and 2-arc of a simple transitive clause would not be neighbors, and the 1-arc successor in a passive would not be a local successor. At the same time, at least for NLs like English, there seems little doubt when one considers facts of coordination, etc., that an example like (i) has the SUPERFICIAL bracketing given:

(i) ⟨⟨The robot⟩ ⟨seized the starlet yesterday⟩⟩

This need not, however, necessarily lead to any fundamental difficulties.

Consider (ii).

(ii) ⟨⟨The starlet⟩ ⟨⟨the robot⟩ ⟨seized yesterday⟩⟩⟩

It is widely agreed that such topicalization sentences have a constituent break after the topic, as given. But this is not generally taken to indicate anything which would be incompatible with an APG VP-less representation of clause structure, because it is in effect assumed that the topic structure is in some sense an overlay on basic clause structures. But, although no one seems to have explored this idea, the possibility exists of a parallel analysis for the main constituent break in cases like (i). Involved would be the hypothesis that the superficial relation borne by *the robot* to the maximal node in (i) is NOT 1 but some nonbasic relation analogous to Topic, which links the initial nominal and the maximal node in (ii). Call this new relation Prime. Hence one possible analysis would treat (i) as involving a Prime-arc foreign successor (see below) of a 1-arc. In these terms, subject-auxiliary inversion cases would be structures in which the final 1-arc does not have a Prime-arc successor, and English would be a V-initial NL even in superficial structures. Unless a view like that just hinted at can be definitively disconfirmed, there is no reason to take the VP-less clause structures of RG and APG representations to be incompatible with the standardly assumed surface bracketings of cases like (i), any more than there is reason to consider them incompatible with the surface bracketing of (ii).

2. The concept of CU structures was developed at the beginning of work on RG; it was in a sense an outgrowth of transformational work on the phenomenon referred to as 'verb raising'; see Aissen (1974a, 1974b), Comrie (1975, 1976). The notion of CU structure has been refined and extended in the RG framework and in APG work; see in particular Aissen and Perlmutter (1976), Johnson and Postal (1980: chapter 8), Gibson (1980), Davies (1981a), Harris (1981), Raposo (1981), Rosen (1983, 1984), Gibson and Raposo (1986), Davies and Rosen (1988), and other citations in Dubinsky and Rosen (1987). Naturally there are diverse and partially inconsistent viewpoints surrounding certain common assumptions here. For a new account of CU structures in APG terms, see Postal (to appear b).

3. The refined CU theory developed in Postal (to appear b) recognizes TWO distinct relations covering the domain previously analyzed in terms of U. One of these is taken

to cover 'causative' type CU structures, the other so-called 'Equi-Clause Union' structures treated in Frantz (1976); see also Johnson and Postal (1980: chapter 8). Adopting this refinement would have no consequences for the current discussion.

4. More precisely, U-arcs which are NOT foreign successors of P-arcs are foreign successors of other U-arcs. This situation arises only in iterated CU structures, that is, where a CU clause is itself embedded as a CU complement. In such a case, the lowest P-arc has a U-arc foreign successor in the middle clause, and that U-arc has a U-arc foreign successor in the highest clause.

5. Arc A is a BRANCH of another B if and only if A's tail and B's head are the same node.

6. This formulation is a simplification in that it ignores arguably CU constructions in various languages like Georgian, Japanese, and Korean, in which the main V and the realization of the complement V form a single surface verbal element. But rather than falsifying the claim in the text, it can be argued that such cases merely reveal the existence of a further layer of structure superimposed on the CU representations so far posited. Consider for example the Georgian example in (i):

(i) = Harris's (1981) (5.1)
masçavlebelma ⟨gadaatargmnina⟩ gelas aḳaḳis leksi
teacher-ERG ⟨he-caused-translate-him-it-II-⟩ Gela-DAT Akaki-GEN poem-NOM
"The teacher made Gela translate Akaki's poem."

This sentence, argued in Harris (1981: chapter 5) to be a CU structure, has a surface form in which the underlying complement V 'translate' is part of a single (bracketed) main clause verbal element. As Harris (1981: 68) puts it: "In Georgian, the matrix verb and the retired verb fuse to form a single word; the matrix verb is realized morphologically as the causative circumfix . . . ." The morphophonological realization of this 'circumfix' is apparently very complicated.

There is a straightforward APG analysis possible for this kind of case. This takes the 'fusing' to be a function of the fact that the U-arc defining CU structures has a successor whose tail is identical to the underlying main clause P-arc head. This would yield schematically (ii).

(ii)

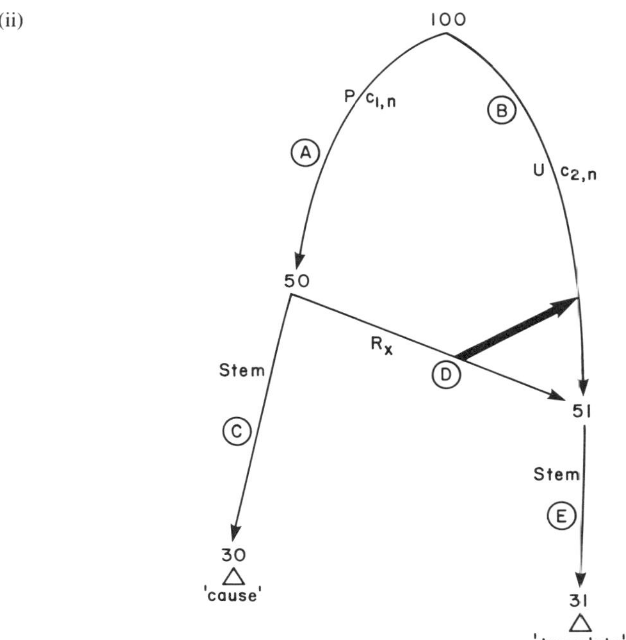

Here arc B has an Rx (foreign) successor, D, which erases it. Since B is erased, it is not a surface arc, while the unerased D is. Hence in the surface form, the element 'translate' is a constituent of the surface predicate, not of the main clause, in accord with the superficial morphological facts. In these terms, the difference between NLs like Georgian, which have single-word CU main V/complement V combinations, and those like French, which do not, is exactly the difference between requiring successor arcs like D in (ii) and not allowing them.

7. Such questions do not arise in other theories, such as that of Gibson and Raposo (1986), which in effect do not recognize the distinction drawn here between CU-image and postimage.

8. However, the converse does not hold. As discussed at some length in Johnson and Postal (1980: chapter 8), some final-stratum complement arcs have (foreign) erasers internal to the complement and thus cannot be launchers. This might be the case, for example, with those final-stratum arcs which sponsor, and are (foreign) erased by, pronominal clitic arc branches of P-arcs in NLs like French; see Johnson and Postal (1980: 329–30), although Postal (to appear a) presents an analysis in which the sponsors of pronominal clitic arcs self-erase.

9. The earliest forerunner of Postimage Principle A seems to be the proposal in Frantz (1977) that all CU complement dependents other than 1s bear the same relations in the main clause as their final relations in the complement. A similar though less general principle was developed by Gibson and Raposo, apparently independently, and

dubbed *the Inheritance Principle* (see Gibson and Raposo 1986), and also by Fauconnier (1983). All of these proposals were made, of course, in context of assumptions not recognizing any distinction between CU-image and postimage.

Combined with other RG and APG laws, Postimage Principle A has certain implications for Oblique-arc (Instrumental, Benefactive, etc.) and 8-arc launchers. In particular, for the latter, both RG and APG have posited laws which would preclude 8-arcs from having postimages. This is assumed in the sentence structures given in what follows. The laws in question do not allow 9-arcs or any other non-Term-arcs to have 8-arc local successors. However, it would be trivial to slightly weaken these laws to allow a non-Term-arc to have an 8-arc local successor if and only if the latter is a postimage. In the case of Oblique arcs, both RG and APG claimed that there were no Oblique local successors. But it would also be trivial to allow Oblique local successors just if these are postimages. This would in effect yield, internal to the current framework, the basic generalization uncovered by Gibson and Raposo (1986); namely, a constituent which is an Oblique_x in a CU complement behaves as an Oblique_x in the main clause.

10. Internal to APG assumptions about the representation of 'coreference' (see (60) in the text below), (42) is oversimplified in a minor way: the claim must hold not only of initial 1-arcs but also of 1-arc anaphoric replacers of initial 1-arcs. Possibly the right condition would be something like (i):

(i) If A is a 1-arc and NOT a local successor, then R2 = 3.

Choice of the right correction for (42) is not relevant to the central issues of this study.

11. Principle (42) is by no means obviously true for French. Most clearly, it requires an account rendering it consistent with the standard situation for intransitive Vs of the type normally taken to involve initial 1s. These behave as 2s and only 2s (hence not as 3s) of the main clause.

(i) a. On l'a fait marcher (, Hervé).
b. *On lui a fait marcher (, à Hervé).
"One/we made Herve walk."

A possible analysis, suggested in effect in Postal (1983b) and Gibson and Raposo (1986), is that *Hervé* in such cases does head a 3-arc in the main clause, but that this has a 2-arc local successor (obligatorily). Another possibility is that (ia) involves complement antipassivization. If so, the final 1-arc would not be an initial arc, and (43) would correctly not be invoked. But see chapter 4, note 13 for an argument against an antipassive view and Postal (to appear b) for fuller discussion. Other problems arise in transitive cases like (ii), under the controversial assumption that these are CIC clauses, a point argued in Postal (1983b, to appear b).

(ii) Hervé les a fait manger cela.
"Herve had them eat that."

In such sentences, whose existence is sometimes overlooked or denied (see chap. 4, note 13), the complement 1 is manifested as an accusative PC in the main clause, indicating that the constituent heading a 1-arc launcher heads a 2-arc in the main clause. Again, consistency with (42) can be maintained via an analysis which allows a 3-arc postimage to have a 2-arc local successor, or in other ways; see sections 4.2 and 4.3.

12. Some principles, either French rules or grammatical laws, must guarantee that

it is always the 3-arc postimage of a 3-arc which has a local successor, since no CIC sentences instantiate a pattern like (i):

(i) Marcel	leur	(des lettres)	(à) Jules
1	3	2	$R_x \neq \{1,2,3\}$
1	9	2	3
1	9	9	9
	3	2	1

This would yield a sentence whose surface structure is identical to (53a) but with the actually impossible meaning, "Marcel had Jules write (letters) to them." The appropriate constraint might say, very roughly, that if one 3-arc postimage A overruns another B, then B is the postimage of a 3-arc. This account is crude, because of the important observation made in Fauconnier (1983) that while cases like (53a) are never interpretable with the PC representing the complement 3, this interpretation is possible in examples like (ii):

(ii) On lui fait téléphoner/envoyer cela.
"One had hir call/send that" or "One had hir called/sent that."

My conclusion is that that the overrun condition described just above only really holds where the 3-arc postimage of a 1-arc has a specified (lexical) head, while on the second readings of (ii) the head is unspecified. See Postal (1985) for some brief discussion.

Chapter Three

1. The analogous assumption is controversial for Romance as a whole; see Radford (1978). Opposition to a passive treatment for French is found in particular in Quicoli (1982: 247–52). And Rosen (1983, 1984) develops an approach to certain CU properties based essentially on a nonpassive analysis of cases like (64b,d); see also Fauconnier (1983) and Legendre (1986).

2. Roughly, the morphology in question is there associated with predicate demotion, that is, local successors for P-arcs. But this is impossible in CU structures, which are defined by U-arc foreign successors of P-arcs. Hence the passive morphology occurs only in non-CU complement (nonreflexive) passives. The rule controlling the relevant phenomena is given in Postal (1985) as:

(i) = English Translation of (60) of Postal (1985)
If A is a predpassive P-arc and not the (foreign) predecessor of a U-arc, then A is the (local) predecessor of a P1 arc.

A reader observes that it is also necessary to block (iii) as a structure for (53a):

(iii) Marcel	leur	(des lettres)	(à) Jules
	$R_x \neq \{1,2,3\}$	2	3
1	3	2	9
1	9	9	9
	1	2	3

For, although (iii) would be consistent with the single reading of (52) under which the PC corresponds to the complement 1, analysis (iii) is inconsistent with the constraints on PC determination needed in French clause union constructions. In particular, since 3s can in general determine PCs, mutatis mutandis, a grammar consistent with analysis

(iii) would allow the impossible reading of (53a) under which the PC corresponds to the complement 3.

3. One unresolved problem is that (66) is not consistent with the account of constraints on 'object raising' given by Legendre (1986) for her variant of French. In that account, the raised nominal is allowed to head only 2-arcs, a condition not met if a nominal like *la voiture* in (66) is raised, which it can be. What I believe to be the correct solution involves a modification of (63) which retains its passive character. This modification depends on the notion of PHANTOM SUCCESSOR, which is a successor which is erased by its predecessor. The approach in question developed only in work begun after the essential completion of this monograph. A structure like (66) may thus be an inadequate stopgap, but one not ultimately that far from adequacy.

4. Structures like (66) also raise problems for a hypothesized law proposed in Perlmutter (to appear), which he refers to as the Non-Initial Demotion Ban. This principle is intended to constrain demotions to term relations. The relevant condition is formulated in Postal (1986b: 350) as in (i):

(i) If A is a Term-arc local successor of B, which outranks A on the hierarchy ($1 < 2 < 3$), then B is NOT a local successor.

Obviously the complement representation in (66) violates (i), since the complement passive 1-arc instantiates variable B in (i), and that arc outranks its 2-arc local successor. To maintain structures like (66) therefore requires some weakening of the proposed principle, possibly something like (i):

(ii) The Weak Demotion Ban
If A is a Term-arc local successor of B, and B is a local successor of C, and B outranks A, then B is a 1-arc and A and C are equivalent (have the same R-sign).

The weaker version allows a restricted class of demotions to term from an advancee status, namely, just those where the demotion is from 1 'back' to an earlier-held relation. The specification that B be a 1-arc eliminates sequences of successive advancements and demotions from 3 to 2 to 3 to 2, etc. The analogous bounding of what Perlmutter calls 'careers' is not needed in the Demotion Ban for 3/2 to 1 to 3/2 to 1, etc., because such careers are already blocked by the 1 Advancement Exclusiveness Law (1AEX). Note that the latter law holds even for CU complements (e.g. in an environment where the Final 1-Arc Law turns out not to hold), and thus even though a potential career like $2 \rightarrow 1 \rightarrow 2 \rightarrow 1$ satisfies the Weak Demotion Ban and the Final 1-Arc Law, it violates the 1AEX and is not a career. On the other hand, the complement career in (66) of the form $2 \rightarrow 1 \rightarrow 2$ satisfies all the relevant principles, since it takes advantage of the possibility allowed by the nonrelevance of the Final 1-Arc Law and avoids a second readvancement to 1. The same weakening also properly allows the structure in (160b) below, one which is entirely independent of both CU structures and passives.

Although (ii) achieves the essential factual goals of Perlmutter's proposal, while maintaining consistency with structures like (66), its extra complexity is suspicious. Notably, the phantom successor approach hinted at in note 3 would not require the expansion of (i) to (ii) to handle (66).

5. The relevant rule might have the form of (i) or of its contrapositive:

(i) Arc-passive (A) → Not (Launcher (A))

An intriguing property of (i) is that it can perhaps be made to predict a puzzling fact, which was noted as early as e.g. Gross (1968: 44), but which has never to my knowledge been accounted for in any framework, namely, reflexive passives (the se-moyen construction) are not embeddable in the CIC:

. . . cependant l'opérateur causatif ne s'applique pas aux transformées moyennes:
Pierre fait, le vin s'achète ici.
*Pierre fait s'acheter le vin ici.

On the standard RG/APG analysis of reflexive passives, see Johnson and Postal (1980: 506–10) and Perlmutter and Postal (1984b: 134–39); these, of course, involve arc-passive arcs and fall under the scope of (i). What remains is only to specify why no structure analogous to (66) in the text with the embedded arc-passive arc having a 2-arc local successor is possible in the case of the reflexive passives.

The answer has to do with the fact that the latter each contain a copy 2-arc, which would be overrun by the 2-arc local successor of the arc-passive arc analogous to that found in (66). This overrun relation would preclude the copy 2-arc from determining a (reflexive) PC under independently needed assumptions. But it is otherwise required in French that reflexive copy 2-arcs and 3-arcs determine PCs; see Postal (to appear a, to appear b) for relevant discussion. The basic claim, however, is that an analogue to (66) for reflexive passives is blocked by the same independently needed principles which preclude (iib) as a parallel to (iia) in the way that (iiib) is parallel to (iiia).

(ii) a. Le cannibale veut se la taper, Marie.
"The cannibal wants to eat Marie."
b. *Le cannibale veut vous taper à lui-même.
"The cannibal wants to eat you."

(iii) a. Le cannibale veut se la décrire, Marie.
"The cannibal wants to describe Marie to himself."
b. Le cannibale veut vous décrire à lui-même.
"The cannibal wants to describe you to himself."

Note that in (iia), which contains a so-called 'inherent reflexive', as in a reflexive passive, and in contrast to (iiia), the reflexive form does NOT correspond to any initial element of the clause. The ill-formedness of (iib) thus strongly suggests there is a principle which would block the grammaticality of an analogue of (66) for reflexive passives. If so, then (i), which is motivated by the postulation of structures like (66), predicts that reflexive passives do not embed in the CIC.

6. Structure (67) differs from previous RG/APG accounts of inversion structures in not recognizing a 'delay' in the advancement of 2 to 1, that is, in having the first coordinate of the 1-arc local successor the same as the first coordinate of the 3-arc local successor. This simpler structure was previously avoided because it appeared to make inversion clauses passive clauses, which was not a desired result. But some positive evidence for the simpler approach arises in the context of the theory of agreement control developed by Aissen (to appear). This leaves the problem of revising the definition of 'Passive Clause' to exclude the case in inversion structures like (67). I will not consider this question here, since its solution apparently involves conceptual changes in relational frameworks; see Perlmutter (1986b); Postal (1987).

7. Potential non-CU cases of inversion in French are discussed below in section 3.4; see also especially Legendre (to appear a, to appear b).

8. The by now large RG/APG literature on unaccusativity includes Davies (1981a), Fauconnier (1983), Harris (1981, 1982), Hubbard (1980, 1981), Olié (1984), Perlmutter (1978, 1983), Perlmutter and Postal (1984a, 1984b), Postal (1984, 1986a), and other references in Dubinsky and Rosen (1987).

9. As is well-known and is illustrated in (68), there is a contrast in past tense auxiliary depending on the main V. Most Vs require the auxiliary *avoir,* but a few intransitives, like *sortir,* require *être*. The examples in (68) illustrate that this distinction does not correlate biconditionally with the unaccusative/unergative distinction. While most intransitives which take *être* are unaccusatives, some unaccusatives, like *disparaître,* take *avoir.* Moreover, some intransitives which take *être,* e.g. *venir (en aide)* 'to help', can be argued to be unergatives.

10. French is sometimes wrongly assumed to lack impersonal passives, an oversight due probably to two facts. First, these structures are used largely in uncolloquial registers. But in these, they are not uncommon. (i), for example, appeared in a French scientific magazine advertisement.

(i) Il a été fait appel, pour la redaction de chacune de ses chapitres, aux meilleurs spécialistes. "Appeal was made, for the writing of each of its chapters, to the best specialists." *La Recherche* 159, October 1984

Second, impersonal passives are for the most part truly impossible even in the relevant styles with ABSOLUTE intransitives, which do not occur with any kind of 'subcategorized' phrase. This class includes French Vs like *dormir* 'to sleep', *marcher* 'to walk', *crier* 'to cry out', etc. This incompatibility with impersonal passives is puzzling, since Vs with such meanings are typically found in impersonal passives in other attested NLs having such constructions.

11. There are claims in the literature which would wrongly entail the nonexistence of sentences like (72e,f), e.g. in Quicoli (1980: 160, 165). As discussed in Postal (1981, 1983) and especially in Postal (1984), these claims ignore the unaccusative/unergative distinction. The relevant restrictions are valid in general only for Vs of the latter category.

12. One can apparently not specify a fully biconditional relation between inversion with nonstandard Vs and CIC complements because of the existence of a limited colloquial construction with *connaître*. See examples like (111a) below.

13. The general principle in question is The Fall-Through Law of Johnson and Postal (1980: 174). Roughly and informally, this says that an arc A which is a member of the c_kth stratum of node ⟨b⟩ is a member of the c_{k+1}th stratum of ⟨b⟩ if and only if there is no arc in the c_{k+1}th stratum which is both distinct from A and erases A. This determines that only having a distinct local eraser keeps an arc in one stratum from also being in the next.

14. The issue here is independent of the contrast between personal and absolute inversion in the complement, since the principles in chapter 2 would determine a main clause 2-arc postimage for the reflexive arc regardless of whether the latter is a final 1-arc local successor of a 2-arc or a final 2-arc. But if the earlier reflexive 2-arc had a 1-arc local successor, then principle RFX1 (= (30)) would be violated in the complement.

15. As shown in (i), there are, independently of any treatment of nonstandard CIC

sentences, limited contexts where a reflexive 2 can appear as a disjunctive pronominal form with no associated PC; see Kayne (1975: 372).

(i) a. *Lucille a décrit(e) elle-même (à Jacques).
"Lucille described herself (to Jacques)."
b. Lucille s'est décrite (à Jacques).
"Lucille described herself (to Jacques)."
c. Lucille s'est décrite à elle-même.
"Lucille described herself to herself."
d. Lucille s'est décrit Jacques.
"Lucille described Jacques to herself."
e. Lucille s'est décrit(*e) elle-même.
"Lucille described herself to herself."

The PC in (ie) is not accusative but dative, determined by a reflexive 3. Were it accusative, the participle would have to show agreement, as in (ib,c). Irrelevantly, when the final *e* is present in (ie), it has a well-formed reading "Lucille described herself herself," in which the reflexive PC is an accusative PC and the postverbal form an emphatic reflexive. So the true reflexive 2 in (ie) is not associated with an accusative PC. Thus, when the 2 and 3 of a French clause are both anaphorically related to its 1, and the 3 is represented by a dative reflexive PC, the reflexive 2 can, exceptionally, appear as a full disjunctive form. This is also possible for some speakers where a reflexive 2 is anteceded by a 3, even if the latter ends up as a 1, namely, those speakers accepting e.g. (19b).

(ii) a. On a décrit Juliette à André.
"One/we described Juliette to Andre."
b. André s'est fait décrire Juliette.
"Andre$_i$ got Juliette described to him$_i$."
c. ?On a décrit lui-même à Andre.
"One/we described Andre to himself."
d. ?Andre s'est fait décrire lui-même.
"Andre got described to himself."

16. An important fact I became aware of only at the end of this research supports the view inherent in the discussion of (83a) that the latter sentence shares a structure with inversion clauses like those in (85), studied in Legendre (to appear a, to appear b). This fact, as far as I know not previously noticed in the literature, is that examples like (83a) remain well-formed when a reflexive PC agreeing with the anaphorically paired nominals appears on the complement V:

(i) a. = (83a) La psychiatrie a fait connaître Marcel à lui-même.
b. La psychiatrie a fait se connaître Marcel à lui-même.
"Psychiatry made Marcel know himself."

The same pattern of optional reflexive PC presence is seen with the cases of (85):

(ii) a. Marcel a nui à lui-même.
b. Marcel s'est nui à lui-même.
"Marcel harmed himself."

Since, as is well-known, a French reflexive PC can appear on a particular V_x only if that PC is anaphorically linked to the final 1 of V_x (see e.g. Y.-C. Morin 1978; Kayne 1975), (ib) requires an analysis in which some nominal anaphorically linked to the *se* is the final 1 of the complement. This condition is met by a personal inversion analysis of the complement of (ib), which is allowed by assumptions already introduced, namely, that *connaître* permits inversion in the complement of *faire,* that reflexive inversion 3s demote to 4 when an initial 2 advances to 1, and that 2-to-1 advancement in CIC inversion complements is optional.

The linkage to a final 1 condition on reflexive PCs required for (ib) would also be met if *(à) lui-même* were regarded as the final 1 of the complement. But this analysis would create two anomalies. First, as already discussed, it would lead to a violation of RFX1 (= (30)). Second, it is otherwise an exceptionless fact that a logically transitive structure with an accusative reflexive PC yields a CIC clause in which the complement 1 is a main clause 2, not a main clause 3 (marked with *à*) like that in (ib).

(iii) a. Jacques se critique.
"Jacques criticizes himself."
b. Cela le fait se critiquer, Jacques.
c. *Cela lui fait se critiquer, à Jacques.
"That makes Jacques criticize himself."

Hence taking *(à) lui-même* to be the final 1 of (ib) is not a viable analysis on two extremely strong grounds. If, however, *Marcel* is the final 1 of the complement of (ib), then that complement cannot be an ordinary transitive clause (whose final 1) would be manifest as a main clause 3. Thus (ib) provides in part a striking independent argument in favor of the inversion hypothesis for *connaître*.

17. As a description of an NL spoken nearly a century ago, it is not surprising that a few points of Johansson's discussion are at variance with the judgments of my consultant. Thus, he claims that the reflexive PC can fail to appear with what I would take to be the unergative Vs *répentir* 'to repent' and *souvenir* 'to remember'. But this is not possible for my consultant.

Incidentally, it is, despite appearances, not difficult to subsume the nonappearance of the reflexive PC with such unergatives under Fauconnier's view that this is a function of nonadvancement to 1. All that is necessary is to see the 'inherent' PCs of these unergatives as a function of the copy advancement of a 2 which itself corresponds to a 2-arc local successor of a 1-arc. In other words, these unergatives are then taken to involve an obligatory type of antipassivization, taking the latter to be defined by the presence of a 2-arc local successor of a 1-arc. In these terms, (ia) would have a structure including (ib).

(i) Hervé se répentira.
"Herve will repent."

(ii)

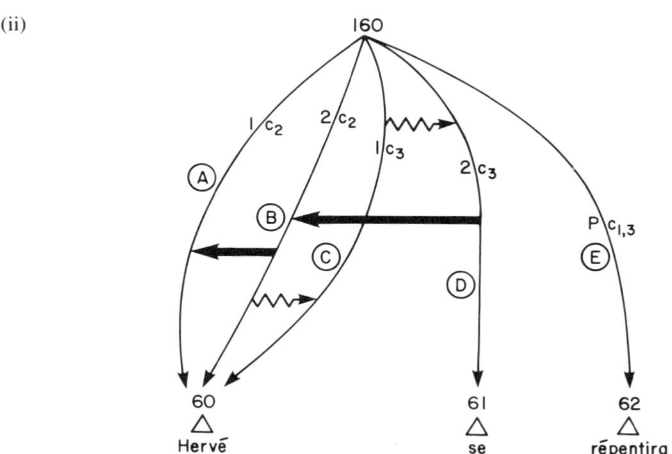

And a sentence like (iii), ungrammatical for my consultant but permissible in the French described by Johansson, would have a structure lacking the local successor B, and hence the copy arc D; see chapter 4, note 36. But that structure can only appear in environments where the Final 1-Arc Law does not require a final 1.

(iii) Cela a fait répentir Hervé.
"That made Herve repent."

18. Constraint (97) ALLOWS certain Vs to occur in clauses lacking final 1s. Evidently any V subject to an 'opposite' constraint, that is, one PRECLUDING occurrence in clauses with final 1s, would not be able to occur in independent clauses. While nothing known precludes such constraints, they will presumably be rather rare, since any V referenced therein would not be able to occur in most clause types, and such Vs are not of much utility.

Chapter Four

1. Notice that the relevant generalization is not capturable in a system, like that of e.g. Chomsky (1981: 103; 1982: 16), which takes the 'agent' phrase of a passive to be base-generated and not a 1 at any level. See the end of chapter 6.

2. Reflexive passives can be formally characterized as a subtype of passive clause in terms of the APG notion of *Copy arc;* see Johnson and Postal (1980: chapter 11) and Postal (1986a: chapter 4). Basically, a copy arc exists when a predecessor/successor pair cosponsor a replacer of the predecessor; see note 36. Such structures share many features with replacers determined by pairs of initial overlapping arcs, those representing 'coreference'. It is thus not surprising that in many NLs, including French, they share the same (reflexive (PC)) morphology.

3. But see Zubizarreta (1985: 253n) for related restrictions on *pour* + infinitive phrases and adverbs like *volontairement*.

4. Ruwet (1982: chapter 6) argues that pairs of copulative phrases like (ia,b) cannot

be regarded as transformationally related with the latter type derived from an underlying structure like the former:

(i) a. Horatio est le meilleur ami d'Hamlet.
"Horatio is the best friend of Hamlet."
b. Le meilleur ami d'Hamlet est Horatio.
"The best friend of Hamlet is Horatio."

But I do not believe that his arguments, which are internal to a certain collection of transformational assumptions, bear on the tenability of the relational proposals about predicate nominal structures suggested in Johnson and Postal (1980) and adopted here.

5. The claim in (105) that the final 1 of predicate nominal constructions like (104b) heads an earlier 2-arc receives support from the distribution of the kind of *en* PC associated with noun complements, e.g. the type in (i):

(i) a. *L'auteur en embauchera Marcel.
"The author of it will hire Marcel."
b. Marcel en embauchera l'auteur.
"Marcel will hire the author of it."
c. L'auteur en sera embauché par Marcel.
"The author of it will be hired by Marcel."
d. *Marcel en sera embauché par l'auteur.
"Marcel will be hired by the author of it."

As the ungrammaticality of *(ia,d) in contrast with the well-formedness of (ib,c) suggests, a condition on such PC occurrences is that the relevant nominal head a 2-arc; see Couquaux (1981) and Pollock (1986) for two recent studies in other frameworks which, in effect, support this restriction. The key fact, then, is that such an *en* can be associated with BOTH the predicate nominal of clauses like (104a) and the 1 linked to the topic of those like (104b).

(ii) a. Marcel en sera la première victime.
"Marcel will be the first victim of it."
b. La première victime en sera Marcel.
"The first victim of it will be Marcel."

Significantly then, under the proposals in the text about predicate nominal constructions, both of these surface nominals head (initial) 2-arcs.

6. Actually, (111b) perhaps has a well-formed reading under which *me* is an accusative PC and the superficial 1 is the initial 1. On that reading, the 1 is personified and the sentence is an irrelevant instance of an ordinary transitive structure.

7. A remark parallel to that made for (111b) holds for (112b), which also has a personification reading "The Boulogne woods know me with pleasure."

8. The word 'remote' applied to an APG relation K (between arcs) refers to the ordinary ancestral of K. The ancestral of a relation R is the relation holding between A and B if A is B, or if A bears R to B, or if A bears R to some C which bears R to B, or, etc. Roughly, the ancestral of R holds between A and B if they are connected by a chain of R relations. See Johnson and Postal (1980) for details.

9. The idea of antipassive analyses of sentences like (113a,b) was introduced in Postal (1977). One argument for such an analysis is that it provides a way of accounting for the fact that essentially these cases alone among CIC structures with transitive complements are such that the final 1 of the complement heads a final 2-arc rather than

a 3-arc in the main clause. The antipassive analysis can account for this by subsuming these cases under Postimage Principle B2 of chapter 2. Other arguments can be developed, having to do particularly with the analysis of reflexive PCs like that of (113b); see Postal (to appear b).

10. 'Outrank' is a predicate defined in Johnson and Postal (1980: 251) which orders arcs according to the position of their R-signs in the sequence:

$$1\ 2\ 3\ \begin{Bmatrix} 8 \\ \text{any Oblique R-sign} \end{Bmatrix}$$

Higher rank is associated with a position further to the left.

11. As seen just below in the text, sentences like (i) arguably involve an adjective *connu*.

(i) Cela est connu de tous (*avec plaisir).

But if, as seems plausible, the *de* phrase here, like those in e.g. (119)–(121), represents a 6-arc local successor of an earlier 1-arc, then the incompatibility with an MA will follow from the rule in (122).

12. My consultant strongly prefers the use of *par* to that of *de* with passives based on *connaître*. This is one aspect of a general tendency to rather narrowly limit passive *de* phrases; so she rejects many instances of them found in the literature.

13. Sentences like (i) raise a potential problem for my treatment of nonstandard sentences:

(i) Cela l'a fait nous connaître/voir.
"That made hir know/see us."

Notably, such sentences, formed with nonstandard Vs, are as acceptable as those like (ii), based on standard complement Vs:

(ii) Cela l'a fait nous critiquer/détester/oublier.
"That made hir criticize/detest/forget us."

While many descriptions of French either ignore sentences like (ii) or propose descriptions which would block them, many grammarians have noted their existence. See Johansson (1896: 100), Sandfeld (1965: 171–72), Grevisse (1969: 1065), Radford (1979: 161–66), Danell (1979: 82–83), Harmer (1979: 212–16), Tasmowski-de Ryck (1984: 404; 1985: 313, 330). Postal (1983b) offers arguments that these sentences are really CIC structures. The key problem is how to keep such sentences compatible with French rule (42a), which provides the 1-arc launcher of transitive complements with a 3-arc postimage, while the accusative PCs in the main clauses of (i) and (ii) indicate that the head of the relevant launcher heads a main clause 2-arc.

My view is that this compatibility is achievable only by recognizing that the predicted 3-arc postimage in the main clause can have a 2-arc local successor. This approach appeals to the phenomenon called 3-TO-2 ADVANCEMENT in the RG/APG literature; see Postal (1986a) for references and discussion of this aspect of clause structure. The only obvious alternative would be to postulate antipassivization in the complement, which would then bypass rule (42) and properly give the final 1-arc of the complement a 2-arc postimage. But it is difficult to make antipassivization compatible with the possibility of the earlier 2 of the complement determining an accusative PC in the complement. For antipassivization would involve a 2-arc local successor B of a 1-arc, with B having a 1-arc local successor, which is the final 1-arc. But B would overrun the only 2-arc which could determine the complement accusative PC in cases like (i) and (ii), precluding that 2-arc from being final. However, the property final is necessary for PC determination, as discussed in Postal (1985, to appear a).

If the 3-to-2 advancement approach is correct, it provides a further argument for the optionality of nonstandard inversion, since only the optionality allows the transitive structure with a nonstandard V to feed rule (42). Notice that one cannot without ad hoc additional statements take cases like (i) to involve 3-to-2 advancement of the 3-arc postimage of an inversion 3-arc. For it is independently clear that advancement to 2 of a 3-arc postimage of a 3-arc is entirely impossible, as shown e.g. by (iii):

(iii) a. Mes hommes lui ont tiré dessus.
"My men shot at hir."
b. Je lui ai fait tirer dessus par mes hommes.
"I had hir shot at by my men."
c. *Je l'ai fait tirer dessus par mes hommes.
"I had hir shot at by my men."

14. For example, one such use corresponds to many English phrases in *for + V-ing*, as in (i):

(i) On a fusillé le président pour avoir accepté des cadeaux très chers.
"The president was shot for having accepted very expensive gifts."

15. But it is not in general true, as Sandfeld claimed, that an *afin de* phrase can always be substituted for a P-Phrase with no loss of grammaticality; see (151) below.

16. Transitive EXI cases like (i) will presumably be in general incompatible with P-Phrases as a consequence of whatever principles preclude this in so many cases for underlying 2s in surface transitive structures. That is, presumably (ia,b) are blocked for the same (so far unspecified) reason.

(i) a. *Il a été caché un enfant par nous pour se protéger contre la revanche.
"A child was hidden by us in order to protect himself against revenge."
b. *Nous avons caché un enfant pour se protéger contre la revanche.
"We hid a child in order to protect himself against revenge."

Moreover, the same principles could then equally block the simple personal passive correspondent of (b) in (c):

c. *Un enfant a été caché par nous pour se protéger contre la revanche.
"A child was hidden by us in order to protect himself against revenge."

For here also the phrase *un enfant* corresponds to the head of an initially accusative 2-arc.

17. As already noted, Zubizarreta describes a variety of French in which (150b) and (151a,b) are ill-formed. Zubizarreta (1985: 253n) claims that the cited ungrammaticality is a function of the fact that " . . . an argument can be interpreted agentively only if it is in subject position." Her idea is apparently that only agents can be associated with the relevant *pour* phrases. So Zubizarreta's view is apparently equivalent to claim (i):

(i) A purposive can only be associated with a final 1.

But this is surely false for both the looser and strict dialects in view of cases like (148), where the purposive is in no case associated with the final 1, which in (148a) is an invisible inanimate relative pronoun linked to *le jeu,* in (148b,c,d) an inanimate referential pronoun, and in (148e) an inanimate dummy pronoun with no reference at all. This conclusion is just reinforced in the looser dialect by cases like (150b) and (151a,b).

18. The V-hood of *voilà* and *voici* was first brought to my attention by David Perlmutter. This status is argued for in Moignet (1974) and Morin (1985). It is supported by the fact that they behave as Vs with respect to compatibility with, and positioning of, the negative elements *ne . . . pas,* PC distribution, enclitics like those in (163), etc.

19. Example (164a) was brought to my attention by David Perlmutter, who first took the enclitic *-il* as an argument for an invisible dummy 1.

20. For discussion of 'brother-in-law' agreement, see Perlmutter (1983), Perlmutter and Zaenen (1984), Aissen (to appear), and many references in Dubinsky and Rosen (1987).

21. The obvious analysis of cases like e.g. (166a,b) would take the initial phrase to be a final and surface 1. But there is some reason to doubt this and to take this phrase to be, like a topic, raised into a higher constituent, with a copy appearing as final 1. One argument for this is that it eliminates the otherwise unique feature of such sentences, namely, the occurrence of a nominal bearing a surface relation R in a clause C even though R has determined a PC on the main V of C. In general, nominals which determine PCs are invisible. But under the analysis suggested, which is consistent in this respect with that advocated in Kayne (1983) in a different framework, the nominal determining the enclitic is an invisible copy pronoun.

22. A key condition on the kind of agreement seen in (163b) is that the 2 determine a PC; it cannot be a full nominal:

(i) Ne voilà-t-il/*-elle pas Marie prisonnière de ses mensonges?
"Isn't Marie a prisoner of her lies?"

23. The V *voici* can never occur in sentences like (163), that is, with an enclitic, a fact with no bearing on present concerns.

24. The force of this observation is attenuated by the fact that this V does not appear to occur in infinitives at all, even of the non-CIC kind:

(i) a. *Il semble lui falloir une voiture.
"It seems hir needs a car."
b. *Il paraît falloir partir.
"It appears to be necessary to leave."

25. The notion Dummy Arc is precisely defined in Johnson and Postal (1980: 404). Here it suffices to take the notion informally as referring to an arc whose head is an 'empty' or dummy nominal. See note 27.

26. An account of the principle underlying this invisibility is sketched in Postal (1986a: chapter 5). Roughly it claims that a French 2-arc headed by a dummy must erase itself if it has no (e.g. 1-arc) local successor. The latter proviso allows the dummy to be manifest in passives like (ib) corresponding to actives like (ia):

(i) a. Je (*le) considère ridicule qu'il ait été embauché.
"I consider it ridiculous that he was hired."
b. Il est considéré ridicule qu'il ait été embauché.
"It is considered ridiculous that he was hired."

27. The notion Ghost (arc) is introduced in Johnson and Postal (1980: chapter 9) as the basic concept characterizing dummy nominals. Roughly, a ghost arc is the 'earli-

est' arc headed by a dummy, that is, the first in a chain of remote successors. Ghosts have single nonoverlapping sponsors, and their R-signs are drawn exclusively from a subset of the Nominal R-signs; see (31). The dummy arcs of note 25 are essentially all and only the remote successors of ghost arcs.

28. The substructure not including the P-Phrase in (185b) has, irrelevantly, an analysis in which *Louis* is an underlying complement 3, not complement 1. This analysis does not combine with the P-Phrase.

29. An open question is why the P-Phrases in (186) cannot be construed with the nominal underlying the PCs *vous*/*nous*. These nominals, being initial nonvedette 2s of the complements, satisfy the conditions in (155). The blockage is presumably due to the as yet obscure constraints which preclude most, but as already stressed not all, association of P-Phrases with underlying accusative 2s. That is, I would try to reduce this fact to the principles operative in *(ia,b,c) of note 16.

30. This is roughly a phenomenon where a genitive arc internal to a nominal has a 3- (or possibly 2-) arc foreign successor. For discussion, see Johnson and Postal (1980), Aissen (1987), and references in Dubinsky and Rosen (1987).

31. However, there appear to be restrictions on the association of an S-Phrase with the EARLIER 1 of a passive. For example, when the final 1 is human, this association appears to be impossible.

(i) Jacques a été giflé par mon père sans le regretter.
"Jacques was slapped by my father without regretting it."

So in (i) the P-Phrase can only be construed with *Jacques*.

32. S-Phrases are perfectly compatible with the postverbal nominal in constructions like (ib):

(i) a. Le jour où Marie est sortie sans vouloir le faire était mercredi.
"The day that Marie went out without wanting to was Wednesday."
b. Le jour où est sortie Marie sans vouloir le faire était mercredi.
"The day that Marie went out without wanting to was Wednesday."

This is consistent with the analysis developed here if, as I believe, *Marie* in such cases heads an 8-arc local successor of a 1-arc, determined by the presence of a self-erasing dummy 1-arc. See Pollock (1986) for discussion of such structures in another framework.

33. An unresolved problem is why the P-Phrase cannot be associated with the final 1, a realization of the earlier 2. This is rather the opposite of the constraint seen in note 31, where it was the final 1/earlier 2 which took precedence.

34. One might ask why reflexive sentences like those in (204) were not appealed to in the discussion of P-Phrases in section 4.2. The answer is that the meanings of such sentences and the meanings of P-Phrases often seem incompatible. Thus, although (i) appears fine, examples like (ii) are very strange or anomalous on semantic grounds.

(i) Il est important de se connaître pour mieux s'apprécier.
"It is important for unspecified$_i$ to know each other in order for unspecified$_i$ to better appreciate each other."

(ii) ???Ces collègues se connaissent pour mieux s'apprecier.
"Those colleagues know each other in order to appreciate each other better."

Facts like those illustrated in (ii) make it difficult to show that a particular failure of a P-Phrase to combine with a nonstandard complement supports the inversion hypothesis.

35. Actually (205b) is STRUCTURALLY ambiguous for many speakers, depending on whether the PC *vous* is a dative or accusative PC. The latter analysis makes the example a sentence of the type discussed in note 13.

36. The notion COPY ARC is defined by Johnson and Postal (1980). Roughly, a copy arc A is an arc cosponsored by a successor/predecessor pair B, C, such that A has the same R-sign and tail node as C, which it erases. Copy arcs are types of replacers. One notable fact about such structures is that the predecessor arc then has at least two distinct realizations—its successor and its copy arc replacer.

37. Rosen (1983, 1984) develops a view under which 2-to-1 advancement is blocked in all CU complements. While possibly well-motivated for Italian, this view seems, despite the arguments of that article, untenable for French in view e.g. of those variants of (207) containing complement reflexive PCs of the sort arguably determined by 2-to-1 advancement.

38. A limitation is required in the framework of chapter 2 since e.g. in examples like (208), the 2-arc of the *faire* clause which is the predecessor of the key arc in the *difficile* clause would have a 9-arc predecessor in that framework. The claim must thus be limited to allow this, which is possible in various straightforward ways; see also chapter 3, note 3.

39. More precisely, there is no way unless the 2-arc sponsored a dummy 2-arc which had a 1-arc local successor. For, as in unembedded EXI cases, this would permit association with a P-Phrase, given rule (155). However, it has already been argued that the dummy 1-arcs associated with EXI constructions in particular are not possible in CIC complements.

40. Sentence (212b) has, of course, an irrelevant well-formed reading under which it means "Marie insulted the director and is going to fire her."

Chapter Five

1. This constraint is even more problematic than so far indicated. For example, there are various forms, including *votre serviteur* 'your servant' and *bibi* 'darling', which, although they have the superficial syntactic properties of third person forms, e.g. with respect to V agreement, are used colloquially in ways SEMANTICALLY equivalent to a first person singular:

(i) Votre serviteur est/*suis content d'être à même de vous aider.
"Your servant (= I) am happy to be in a position to help you."

(ii) Bibi en a/*ai marre d'attendre.
"Darling (= I) am fed up with waiting."

But these forms can appear as final 1s of reflexive passives with their first person interpretations:

(iii) Votre serviteur ne se trahit pas.
"One doesn't betray me."

(iv) Bibi ne se trahit pas.
"One doesn't betray me."

This would seem to indicate that the constraint should in some way reference the non–third person morphology. But, inconsistent with this is the fact that the use of *on* where it represents a first person plural is incompatible with the reflexive passive interpretation, even though *on* is, of course, morphologically third person:

(v) (Nous), on a/*avons voulu partir.
"We wanted to leave."

(vi) (Nous), on ne se trahit pas.
"We don't betray ourselves/each other," *"One can't betray us."

An account of the reflexive passive person constraint which has just these consequences is anything but obvious.

2. Zribi-Hertz (1982: 363–65) ends up rejecting the existence of a syntactic constraint to third person 1s on reflexive passives, arguing that the restrictions involve complex semantic/pragmatic factors. She cites (p. 365) example (i) to show that reflexive passives are, in the right context, possible with non–third person final 1s:

(i) Vous allez voir, je me transporte facilement. Je suis la perle des paralytiques.
"You'll see, I transport easily. I am the pearl of paralytics."

But my consultant finds this extremely forced. It is unclear how important this question is for current purposes, since the contrast between (221) and (222) remains.

3. Related but in some sense 'opposite' principles may underlie other special cases of predicate agreement in both French and English. I refer to forms like (i):

(i) It is I who AM under investigation.

(ii) C'est moi qui SUIS le plus en danger.
"It is I who am the most in danger."

In such examples, the subordinate clause, which seems linked to the predicate nominal 1, which is third person, nonetheless shows first person agreement under the influence of the first person predicate nominals. Taking this agreement to be a function of the character of the relative pronouns, one can suspect that there is some principle allowing an anaphor linked to the 1 of a predicate nominal construction to take on a morphological analysis appropriate for an anaphor linked to the predicate nominal. Apparently this phenomenon, unlike the 'opposite' one, is not related to counterfactuality. If the two sorts of phenomena, that in the text and that in (i) and (ii), are indeed special cases of some general property, it would appear that one needs a theory of ways in which anaphor morphology determination can be 'transferred' from one nominal A to another B when these stand in certain relationships.

Chapter Six

1. It is possible, therefore, that in some NLs, ALL of what appear to be CU structures with transitive complements involving 3-arc postimages of 1-arc launchers are actually cases of complement inversion, either personal, absolute, or indifferently either.

2. A quite revealing work in connection with this claim is Wehrli (1983: 182), which gives familiar data like (i) and (ii) parallel to (7) illustrating the constraint referred to here as 'FC':

(i) = Wehrli's (3)

a. Jean le fait embrasser ⟨e⟩ ⟨$_S$ à Marie⟩
"Jean makes Marie kiss him (him = Jean)."

b. *Jean nous fait embrasser ⟨e⟩ ⟨$_S$ à Marie⟩
"Jean makes Marie kiss us."

(ii) = Wehrli's (4)

a. Jean le fait épouser ⟨e⟩ ⟨$_S$ à Marie⟩
"Jean makes Marie marry him."

b. *Jean te fait épouser ⟨e⟩ ⟨$_S$ à Marie⟩
"Jean makes Marie marry you."

(iii) = Wehrli's (5)
⟨S Jean fait V NP ⟨$_S$ à Marie⟩⟩

Wehrli claims that since the pairs in (i) and (ii) have essentially identical structures and (transformational) derivations, the principle distinguishing them must refer to the different PCs themselves. "In both (3) and (4), there is a sharp contrast between examples (a) and (b), although the structure is exactly the same, namely the one given in (5). The derivation is the same as well." To account for the ill-formedness of (ib) and (iib), Wehrli then proposes what he calls 'Principle P':

(iv) Principle P
A clitic of the class C attached to the complex *faire* à V_{inf} is interpreted as the subject of V_{inf}, where C is the class of clitics that can be +dative, i.e. *me, te, se, nous, vous, lui, leur.*

However, a comparison of Principle P as a basis for the FC constraints with an account incorporating FC plus the inversion hypothesis quickly reveals the inferiority of the former and in fact, its factual untenability. First, Principle P is in all known dialects of French flat out incompatible with the unchallenged existence of any nonstandard sentences, an existence Wehrli (1983) does not mention. Second, variants of French in which Principle P is clearly false INDEPENDENTLY of nonstandard Vs nonetheless have all the other properties this is supposed to characterize. Thus there are many speakers, including my principal consultants, who accept examples like (v); see Postal (1984):

(v) a. Hervé me lui a fait envoyer cela.
"Herve had me send that to hir."

b. Hervé me la lui a fait envoyer.
"Herve had me send it to hir."

c. Hervé me lui a laissé téléphoner.
"Herve let me call hir."

The relevant sentences are clearly instances of what Wehrli calls 'the complex *faire* à V_{inf}'. Yet the dative PC *lui* is obviously NOT interpreted as the 1 of the infinitive, but as its 3. Third, unlike the inversion approach, Principle P offers absolutely no account of the correlations between FC and other apparent anomalies with nonstandard Vs. I conclude that a claim that a PC of Wehrli's class C must be interpreted as a 1 of the complement is untenable and hence irrelevant to the facts involving FC. Thus Wehrli's Principle P is not a serious alternative to FC = (56) combined with the inversion hypothesis.

3. A claim of methodological impermissibility for the inversion analysis advocated here could, I believe, be based on the kind of reasoning found in Cole and Sridhar (1977: 705, n. 8). Postal (1982: 417, 40n) attempts to show that their methodological strictures have no genuine force.

4. The formulation in (233) artifically ignores the existence of sentences like (111a).

5. Frantz's proposal fails for French because it would claim that what appear to be standard transitive complements are actually personal inversion clauses. But this

allows no basis for the contrasts seen throughout this study to separate standard from nonstandard complements and to support an inversion structure ONLY for the latter.

6. I am indebted to Yael Ravin for clarifying my understanding of the relevant GB assumptions.

7. The GB assumption that every position strictly subcategorized by *a* must be theta-marked by *a* is argued to be untenable on entirely different grounds in Postal and Pullum (to appear) and Pullum (to appear).

References

Aissen, Judith. 1974a. "The Syntax of Causative Constructions." Ph.D. diss., Harvard University. A revised version is published as *The Syntax of Causative Constructions,* New York: Garland, 1979.

———. 1974b. "Verb Raising," *Linguistic Inquiry* 5: 325–66.

———. 1987. *Tzotzil Clause Structure.* Dordrecht, Holland: D. Reidel.

———. To appear. "Towards a Theory of Agreement Controllers." In Postal and Joseph, to appear.

Aissen, Judith, and David M. Perlmutter. 1976. "Clause Reduction in Spanish." In *Proceedings of the Second Annual Meeting of the Berkeley Linguistics Society,* Berkeley, California. Revised version in Perlmutter 1983.

Anderson, Stephen R. 1984. "On Representations in Morphology: Case Marking, Agreement, and Inversion in Georgian." *Natural Language and Linguistic Theory* 2: 157–218.

Authier, Jacqueline. 1972. *Etude sur les formes passives du français.* Documentation et recherche en linguistique allemande contemporaine. Vincennes, Université de Paris, 8.

Bach, Emmon. 1981. "Discontinuous Constituents in Generalized Categorial Grammars." In *Proceedings of the Eleventh Annual Meeting of the North Eastern Linguistic Society.* Department of Linguistics, University of Massachusetts, Amherst, Massachusetts.

Bell, Sarah J. 1974. "Two Consequences of Advancement Rules in Cebuano." In *Papers from the Fifth Annual Meeting of the North Eastern Linguistic Society,* Harvard University, Cambridge, Massachusetts.

———. 1976. "Cebuano Subjects in Two Frameworks." Ph.D. diss., MIT.

Bordelois, Ivonne A. 1980. "Review of *French Syntax: The Transformational Cycle,* by R. Kayne." *Language* 56: 146–57.

Brame, Michael K. 1978. *Base-Generated Syntax.* Seattle: Noit Amrofer.

———. 1979. *Essays Toward Realistic Syntax.* Seattle: Noit Amrofer.

———. 1980. *Essays on the General Theory of Binding and Fusion.* Seattle: Noit Amrofer.

———. 1981. "Trace Theory With Filters vs. Lexically Based Syntax Without." *Linguistic Inquiry* 12: 275–93.

Burston, Jack L. 1979. "The Pronominal Verb Construction in French." *Lingua* 48: 147–76.

Cannings, Peter, and Marvin D. Moody. 1978. "A Semantic Approach to Causation in French." *Lingvisticae Investigationes* 2: 331–62.

Chomsky, Noam. 1981. *Lectures on Government and Binding*. Dordrecht, Holland: Foris.

———. 1982. *Some Concepts and Consequences of the Theory of the Theory of Government and Binding*. Cambridge, Massachusetts: MIT Press.

Cole, Peter, and S. N. Sridhar. 1977. "Clause Union and Relational Grammar: Evidence from Hebrew and Kannada." *Linguistic Inquiry* 8: 700–713.

Comrie, Bernard. 1975. "Causatives and Universal Grammar." *Transactions of the Philological Society 1974:* 1–32.

———. 1976. "The Syntax of Causative Constructions: Cross-Language Similarities and Divergences." In M. Shibatani, ed., *The Grammar of Causative Constructions.* New York: Academic Press.

Cook, Eung-Do, and Donna B. Gerdts, eds. 1984. *Syntax and Semantics 16: The Syntax of Native American Languages*. New York: Academic Press.

Cooper, Robin. 1983. *Quantification and Syntactic Theory*. Dordrecht, Holland: D. Reidel.

Couquaux, Daniel. 1981. "French Predication and Linguistic Theory." In May and Koster 1981.

Couquaux, Daniel, and Mitsou Ronat, eds. 1986. *La grammaire modulaire*. Paris: Editions de Minuit.

Danell, Karl J. 1979. *Remarques sur la construction dite causative*. Stockholm: Almqvist and Wiksell.

Davies, William D. 1981a." Choctaw Clause Structure." Ph.D. diss., University of California at San Diego, La Jolla, California; a revised version is published as *Choctaw Verb Agreement and Universal Grammar,* Dordrecht, Holland: D. Reidel, 1986.

———. 1981b. "Choctaw Subjects and Multiple Levels of Syntax." In Hoekstra, van der Hulst, and Moortgat 1981.

———. 1984. "Choctaw Switch Reference and Levels of Syntactic Representation." In Cook and Gerdts, 1984.

Davies, William D., and Carol Rosen. 1988. "Unions as Multi-Predicate Clauses." *Language* 64: 52–88.

Davis, Steven, and Marianne Mithun, eds. 1979. *Linguistics, Philosophy, and Montague Grammar.* Austin: University of Texas Press.

Dorel, Martine. 1977. "The Two Verbs *Faire* in French Expressions of Causation." MIT, Cambridge, Massachusetts.

———. 1980. "The Two Verbs *Faire* in French Expressions of Causation." In Frank Nussel, ed., *Contemporary Studies in Romance Languages*. Bloomington: Indiana University Linguistics Club.

Dowty, David R. 1978. "Governed Transformations as Lexical Rules in a Montague Grammar." *Linguistic Inquiry* 9: 393–426.

———. 1979. "Dative 'Movement' and Thomason's Extensions of Montague Grammar." In Davis and Mithun 1979.

———. 1982a. "Grammatical Relations and Montague Grammar." In Jacobson and Pullum 1982.

———. 1982b. "More on the Categorical Analysis of Grammatical Relations." In Zaenen 1982.

Dryer, Matthew. 1982. "Passive and Inversion in Kannada." In *Proceedings of the Eighth Annual Meeting of the Berkeley Linguistics Society,* Berkeley, California.

Dubinsky, Stanley, and Carol Rosen. 1987. "A Bibliography on Relational Grammar through May 1987 with Selected Titles on Lexical Functional Grammar." Bloomington, Indiana: Indiana University Linguistics Club.

Dubois, Jean. 1967. *Grammaire structurale du français: le verbe.* Paris: Librairie Larousse.

Dunbar, Richard Terry. 1981. "The Obligatory Use of the Preposition à Plus Disjunctive Pronoun After Certain Verbs in French." Ph.D. diss., University of Illinois, Urbana, Illinois.

Emonds, Joseph. 1978. "Le groupe verbal composé V′ V en français." In *Syntaxe et sémantique du français. Cahier de linguistique Numéro 8.*

Fauconnier, Gilles. 1974. *La coréférence: Syntaxe ou sémantique?* Paris: Editions du Seuil.

———. 1983. "Generalized Union." In Tasmowski-de Ryck and Willems 1983.

Frantz, Donald. 1976. "Equi-Subject Clause Union." In *Proceedings of the Second Annual Meeting of the Berkeley Linguistics Society,* Berkeley, California.

———. 1977. "Downstairs Transitivity in Causative Clause Unions." In *Work Papers of the Summer Institute of Linguistics,* 21. University of North Dakota.

Gaatone, David. 1976a. "Les pronoms conjoints dans la construction factitive." *Revue de linguistique romane* 40: 165–82.

———. 1976b. "L'alternance *à/par* dans les constructions causatives (factitives)." *Actes du 13e Congrès de Linguistique et Philologie romanes.* Quebec.

Gazdar, Gerald. 1981a. "On Syntactic Categories." *Philosophical Transactions (Series B) of the Royal Society* 295: 267–83.

———. 1981b. "Unbounded Dependencies and Coordinate Structure." *Linguistic Inquiry* 12: 155–84.

———. 1982. "Phrase Structure Grammar." In Jacobson and Pullum 1982.

Gazdar, Gerald, Ewan Klein, Geoffrey K. Pullum, and Ivan A. Sag. 1985. *Generalized Phrase Structure Grammar.* Oxford: Basil Blackwell.

Gazdar, Gerald, Geoffrey K. Pullum, and Ivan A. Sag. 1982. "Auxiliaries and Related Phenomena in a Restrictive Theory of Grammar." *Language* 58: 591–638.

Gerdts, Donna B. To appear. "Revaluation and Inheritance in Korean Causative Union." In Postal and Joseph (to appear).

Gibson, Jeanne. 1980. "Clause Union in Chamorro and in Universal Grammar." Ph.D. diss., University of California at San Diego, La Jolla, California.

Gibson, Jeanne, and Eduardo Raposo. 1986. "Clause Union, the Stratal Uniqueness Law, and the Chômeur Relation." *Natural Language and Linguistic Theory* 4: 295–332.

Gonzalez, Nora Martinez. 1985. "Object and Raising in Spanish." Ph.D. diss., University of California at San Diego, La Jolla, California.

———. 1986. "Interaction of Inversion and Clause Union in Spanish." In *Proceedings of the Second Eastern States Conference on Linguistics,* State University of New York, Buffalo, New York.

———. To appear. "The Unaccusativity of Spanish Raising Predicates." In Postal and Joseph (to appear).

Grevisse, Maurice. 1969. *Le bon usage*. Gembloux, Belgium: Editions J. Duculot.

Gross, Maurice. 1968. *Grammaire transformationnelle du français: syntaxe du verbe*. Paris: Librairie Larousse.

———. 1975. *Méthodes en syntaxe*. Paris: Hermann.

Harmer, L. C. 1979. *Uncertainties in French Grammar.* Cambridge: Cambridge University Press.

Harris, Alice. 1981. *Georgian Syntax: A Study in Relational Grammar.* Cambridge: Cambridge University Press.

———. 1982. "Georgian and the Unaccusative Hypothesis." *Language* 58: 290–306.

———. 1984a. "Case Marking, Verb Agreement, and Inversion in Udi." In Perlmutter and Rosen 1984.

———. 1984b. "Inversion as a Rule of Universal Grammar: Georgian Evidence." In Perlmutter and Rosen 1984.

Hendrick, Randall. 1978. "The Post-Cyclicity of Clitic Placement and the *Faire* Construction in French." In *Syntaxe et sémantique du français Cahier de linguistique numéro 8*.

Herschensohn, Julia. 1981. "French Causatives: Restructuring, Opacity, Filters, and Construal." *Linguistic Analysis* 8: 217–80.

Hoekstra, Teun, Harry van der Hulst, and Michael Moortgat, eds. 1981. *Perspectives on Functional Grammar.* Dordrecht, Holland: Foris.

Hubbard, Phillip L. 1980. *The Syntax of the Albanian Verb Complex*. Ph.D. diss., University of California at San Diego, La Jolla, California.

———. 1981. "Dative Clitics in Albanian: Evidence for Syntactic Levels." In *Proceedings of the Seventh Annual Meeting of the Berkeley Linguistics Society,* Berkeley, California.

———. 1982. "Albanian Reflexives: Violations of Proposed Universals." Ohio University, Athens, Ohio.

Hyman, Laurence, and Karl Zimmer. 1976. "Imbedded Topic in French." In Li 1976.

Jackson, Charles H. 1982. "Multi-Level Syntactic Description: Evidence from Tamil." In *Working Papers in Relational Grammar,* Department of Linguistics, University of California at San Diego, La Jolla, California.

Jacobson, Pauline, and Geoffrey K. Pullum, eds. 1982. *The Nature of Syntactic Representation*. Dordrecht, Holland: D. Reidel.

Johansson, Alfred. 1896. "Etude syntaxique sur le verbe *faire* en français moderne." In *Mélanges de Philologie Romane dediés à Carl Wahlund.* Macon: Protat frères.

Johnson, David E., and Paul M. Postal. 1980. *Arc Pair Grammar.* Princeton: Princeton University Press.

Kayne, Richard S. 1975. *French Syntax*. Cambridge: MIT Press.
———. 1983. "Chains, Categories External to S, and French Complex Inversion." *Natural Language and Linguistic Theory* 1: 107–39.
Le Bidois G., and R. Le Bidois. 1968. *Syntaxe du français moderne*. Paris: A. and J. Picard.
Legendre, Géraldine. 1986. "Object Raising in French: A Unified Account." *Natural Language and Linguistic Theory* 4: 137–84.
———. To appear a. "French Inversion Structures." In Postal and Joseph (to appear).
———. To appear b. "Topics in French Syntax." Ph.D. diss., University of California at San Diego.
Li, Charles, ed. 1976. *Subject and Topic*. New York: Academic Press.
Marlett, Stephen A. 1984. "Switch-Reference and Subject-Raising in Seri." In Cook and Gerdts 1984.
Martinon, Phillipe. 1927. *Comment on parle en français*. Paris: Librairie Larousse.
May, Robert, and Jan Koster, eds. 1981. *Levels of Syntactic Representation*. Dordrecht, Holland: Foris.
McA'Nulty, Judith. 1978. "Les transformations d'extraction, les contraintes qui en rendent compte, et la non-trivialité des problèmes résiduels." In *Syntaxe et sémantique du français. Cahier de linguistique numéro 8*.
Melis, Ludo, Liliane Tasmowski, Paul Verluyten, and Dominique Willems. 1985. *Les constructions de la phrase française. Studies in Language 3, Communication and Cognition*. Ghent, Belgium.
Milner, Jean-Claude. 1982. *Ordres et raisons de langue*. Paris: Editions du Seuil.
Moignet, Gérard. 1974. *Etudes de psycho-systématique française*. Paris: Editions Klincksieck.
Morin, Jean-Yves. 1978. "Une théorie interprétative des causatives en français." *Lingvisticae Investigationes* 2: 363–417.
Morin, Yves Charles. 1977. "Une réanalyse des constructions en *faire*." University of Montreal, Montreal, Canada.
———. 1978. "Interprétation des pronoms et des réfléchis en français." In *Syntaxe et sémantique du français. Cahier de Linguistique 8*. Montreal: Presses de l'Université de Montréal.
———. 1985. "On the Two French Subjectless Verbs *Voici* and *Voilà*. Language 61: 777–820.
Olié, Annie. 1984. "L'hypothèse de l'inaccusatif en français." *Lingvisticae Investigationes* 8: 363–401.
Perlmutter, David M. 1978. "Impersonal Passives and the Unaccusative Hypothesis." *Proceedings of the Fourth Annual Meeting of the Berkeley Linguistics Society,* University of California, Berkeley.
———. 1980. "Relational Grammar." In *Syntax and Semantics 13*. New York: Academic Press.
———. 1982. "Syntactic Representation, Syntactic Levels, and the Notion of Subject." In Jacobson and Pullum 1982.
———. 1983. "Personal Versus Impersonal Constructions." *Natural Language and Linguistic Theory* 1: 141–200.

———. 1984. "Working 1s and Inversion in Italian, Japanese, and Quechua." In Perlmutter and Rosen 1984.

———. 1986a. "Some Consequences of the Unaccusative Hypothesis for the Theory of Clause Union." Paper presented at North Eastern Linguistics Society, MIT, Cambridge, Massachusetts.

———. 1986b. "Toward Basis Grammar." Paper presented at the annual meeting of the Linguistic Society of America, New York, New York.

———. To appear. "Successor Objects, the Demotion Ban, and the Class of Careers."

Perlmutter, David M., ed. 1983. *Studies in Relational Grammar 1*. Chicago: University of Chicago Press.

Perlmutter, David M., and Paul M. Postal. 1983. "Some Laws of Basic Clause Structure." In Perlmutter 1983.

———. 1984a. "The 1-Advancement Exclusiveness Law." In Perlmutter and Rosen 1984.

———. 1984b. "Impersonal Passives and Some Relational Laws." In Perlmutter and Rosen 1984.

Perlmutter, David M., and Carol G. Rosen, eds. 1984. *Studies in Relational Grammar 2*. Chicago: University of Chicago Press.

Perlmutter, David M., and Annie Zaenen. 1984. "The Indefinite Extraposition Construction in Dutch and German." In Perlmutter and Rosen 1984.

Pollock, Jean-Yves. 1986. "Sur la syntaxe de *en* et le paramètre du sujet nul." In Couquaux and Ronat 1986.

Postal, Paul M. 1977. "Antipassive in French." *Lingvisticae Investigationes* 1: 333–74.

———. 1981. "A Failed Analysis of the French Cohesive Infinitive Construction." *Linguistic Analysis* 8: 281–323.

———. 1982. "Some Arc Pair Grammar Descriptions." In Jacobson and Pullum 1982.

———. 1983a. "On Characterizing French Grammatical Structure." *Linguistic Analysis* 11: 361–417.

———. 1983b. "A French Construction Which Isn't What It Seems." Thomas J. Watson Research Center, IBM, Yorktown Heights, New York.

———. 1984. "French Indirect Object Cliticization and SSC/BT." *Linguistic Analysis* 14: 111–72.

———. 1985. "La dégradation de prédicat et un genre négligé de montée." *Recherches Linguistiques* 13: 33–68.

———. 1986a. *Studies of Passive Clauses*. Albany: State University of New York Press.

———. 1986b. "Why Irish Raising Is Not Anomalous." *Natural Language and Linguistic Theory* 4: 333–56.

———. 1987. "Some Revisions of Arc Grammar." Paper presented at the Third Biennial Conference on Relational Grammar and Grammatical Relations, University of Iowa, Iowa City, Iowa.

———. To appear a. "French Indirect Object Demotion." In Postal and Joseph (to appear).

———. To appear b. *French Indirect Objects*.

Postal, Paul M., and Brian Joseph, eds. To appear. *Studies in Relational Grammar: 3*.

Postal, Paul M., and Geoffrey K. Pullum. To appear. "Expletive Noun Phrases in Subcategorized Positions."
Pullum, Geoffrey K. To appear. "Extraposed Irrealis Clauses in English." In *Proceedings of the Fourth Eastern States Conference on Linguistics,* Ohio State University, Columbus, Ohio.
Quicoli, A. Carlos. 1980. "Clitic Movement in French Causatives." *Linguistic Analysis* 6: 131–85.
———. 1982. "Some Issues on the Theory of Clitics." *Linguistic Analysis* 8: 203–73.
Radford, Andrew. 1978. "Agentive Causatives in Romance: Accessibility Versus Passivisation." *Journal of Linguistics* 14: 35–58.
———. 1979. "Clitics Under Causatives in Romance." *Journal of Italian Linguistics* 1: 137–81.
Raposo, Eduardo José Buzaglo Paiva. 1981. "A Construção ⟨⟨União de Orações⟩⟩ na Gramática do Português." Ph.D. diss., University of Lisbon, Lisbon, Portugal.
Roberts, James Stewart. 1980. "French Causatives in Generative Syntax." Ph.D. diss., Georgetown University.
Rosen, Carol G. 1983. "Universals of Causative Union: A Co-Proposal to the Gibson-Raposo Typology." In *Papers from the Nineteenth Regional Meeting of the Chicago Linguistics Society,* Chicago, Illinois.
———. 1984. "Chômeur Causees and the Universals of Causative Union." In *Cornell University Working Papers in Linguistics* 5: 179–98.
Rouveret, Alain, and Jean-Roger Vergnaud. 1980. "Specifying Reference to the Subject." *Linguistic Inquiry* 11: 97–202.
Ruwet, Nicolas. 1972. *Théorie syntaxique et syntaxe du français.* Paris: Editions du Seuil.
———. 1982. *Grammaire des insultes et autres études.* Paris: Editions du Seuil.
Sag, Ivan A. 1982. "A Semantic Theory of 'NP-movement' Dependencies." In Jacobson and Pullum 1982.
———. 1983. "On Parasitic Gaps." *Linguistics and Philosophy* 6: 35–45.
Sandfeld, Karl. 1928. *Syntaxe du français contemporain 1.* les pronoms. Paris: Librairie Honoré Champion.
———. 1965. *Syntaxe du français contemporain: l'infinitif.* Geneva: Librairie Droz.
Seuren, Pieter A. M. 1972. "Predicate Raising and Dative in French and Sundry Languages." Magdalen College, Oxford.
Taraldsen, Knut T. 1981. "Remarks on Government, Thematic Structure, and the Distribution of Empty Categories." In May and Koster 1981.
Tasmowski-de Ryck, Liliane. 1983. "L'immixtion causative." *Travaux de Linguistique* 9–10: 103–26.
———. 1984. "?*Lui faire téléphoner quelqu'un d'autre: une stratégie?" *Lingvisticae Investigationes* 8: 403–27.
———. 1985. "Faire infinitif." In Melis, Tasmowski, Verluyten, and Willems 1985.
Tasmowski-de Ryck, Liliane, and Dominique Willems, eds. 1983. *Problems in Syntax, Communication, and Cognition.* Ghent, Belgium: Plenum.
Wehrli, Eric. 1983. "Remarks on Cliticization in French Causatives." *MIT Working Papers in Linguistics* 5: 180–95.

Zaenen, Annie, ed. 1982. *Subjects and Other Subjects: Proceedings of the Harvard Conference on the Representation of Grammatical Relations.* Bloomington, Indiana: Indiana University Linguistics Club.

Zribi-Hertz, Anne. 1982. "La construction 'se moyen' du français et son statut dans le triangle: Moyen-passif-réfléchi." *Lingvisticae Investigationes* 6: 345–401.

Zubizarreta, Maria Luisa. 1985. "The Relation between Morphophonology and Morphosyntax: The Case of Romance Causatives." *Linguistic Inquiry* 16: 247–89.

Index